The Family Therapy Collections

James C. Hansen, Series Editor

Douglas C. Breunlin, Volume Editor

STAGES: PATTERNS OF CHANGE OVER TIME

AN ASPEN PUBLICATION®
Aspen Systems Corporation
Rockville, Maryland
Royal Tunbridge Wells
1985

SCHOOL OF
CALIFORNIA PROFESSIONAL PSYCHOLOGY
LOS ANGELES

Library of Congress Cataloging in Publication Data
Main entry under title:

Stages, patterns of change over time.

(The Family therapy collections, ISSN 0735-9152 ; 14)
"An Aspen publication."
Includes bibliographies and index.
1. Family psychotherapy. 2. Family psychotherapy —
Methodology. I. Breunlin, Douglas C. II. Series.
RC488.5.S73   1985   616.89'156   85-9081
ISBN: 0-89443-614-7

Editorial Services: Ruth McKendry

The Family Therapy Collections series is indexed in *Psychological Abstracts* and the PsycINFO database

Library of Congress Catalog Card Number: 85- 9081
ISBN: 0-89443-614-7
ISSN: 0735-9152

Printed in the United States of America

1 2 3 4 5

To my mother
and father
D.C.B.

Table of Contents

Board of Editors vii

Contributors ix

Series Preface xi

Preface xiii

Acknowledgments xvii

1. Expanding the Concept of Stages in Family Therapy 1
    Douglas C. Breunlin
    Expanding the Meaning of Stages 3
    The Stages of Family Therapy 7

2. Beginning Family Therapy 16
    Rocco A. Cimmarusti and Jay Lappin
    Creation of Workable Realities 18
    Out-of-Session Issues 21
    In-Session Issues 23

3. The Middle Phase: The Evolving Process of Change 26
    Dennis McGuire
    Definition and Parameters 27
    Formula for Change in the Middle Phase 27
    Conclusion 32

4. Ending Family Therapy: Some New Directions 33
    Anthony W. Heath
    Termination in Medical Practice 34

Indications and Contraindications 35
Application of the Medical Practice Model 36
Conclusion 39

5. The Stages of Structural Family Therapy 41
    Betty M. Karrer and John Schwartzman
    Spatial and Temporal Dimensions 42
    Theoretical Assumptions of the Structural Family
        Therapy Model 42
    From Assumptions to Stages 43
    The Broader Temporal Dimension 46

6. The Stages of Strategic Family Therapy 51
    Judith Mazza
    Issues in Staging Strategic Therapy 51
    Variables that Define the Stage of Therapy 53
    Case Study: The Daughter Who Thought She Could
        Not Be a Wife 54
    Conclusion 60

7. Stages of Family Therapy with Divorcing Families 62
    Virginia A. Simons and Douglas H. Sprenkle
    A Perspective 62
    A Framework for the Divorcing Family 64
    General Principles 64
    Stages of Divorce Treatment 67

8. Stages of Family Therapy with Severely Disturbed Adolescents . 75
    Susan K. Mackey
    Guidelines 77
    Stages 78
    Conclusion 85

9. Has Family Therapy Reached the Stage Where It Can
        Appreciate the Concept of Stages? 88
    Richard C. Schwartz
    The Stages of Discovery 88
    The Field of Family Therapy 90
    Models of Family Therapy 91
    Individual Family Therapists 92
    Conclusion 94

Index 95

Board of Editors

Board of Editors

(continued)

Contributors

Volume Editor

DOUGLAS C. BREUNLIN

DOUGLAS C. BREUNLIN
Institute for Juvenile Research
Chicago, Illinois

ROCCO CIMMARUSTI
The Depot/Center for Family
Development
Chicago, Illinois

ANTHONY W. HEATH
Lombard, Illinois

BETTY M. KARRER
Institute for Juvenile Research
Chicago, Illinois

JAY LAPPIN
Philadelphia Child Guidance Clinic
Philadelphia, Pennsylvania

DENNIS MCGUIRE
Kenosha, Wisconsin

SUSAN K. MACKEY
Associates in Adolescent Psychiatry
Skokie, Illinois

JUDITH MAZZA
The Family Therapy Institute of
Washington, D.C.
Rockville, Maryland

RICHARD C. SCHWARTZ
Institute for Juvenile Research
Chicago, Illinois

JOHN SCHWARTZMAN
Center for Family Studies/The Family
Institute
Chicago, Illinois

VIRGINIA A. SIMONS
Isaac Ray Center, Inc.
Chicago, Illinois

DOUGLAS H. SPRENKLE
Purdue University
West Lafayette, Indiana

Series Preface

The *Family Therapy Collections* is a quarterly publication in which topics of current and specific interest to family therapists are presented. Each volume contains articles authored by practicing professionals, providing in-depth coverage of a single significant aspect of family therapy. This volume focuses on the stages in the process of family therapy.

Social scientists have described stages in individual development and the family life cycle as well as stages in individual and group therapy. However, only an occasional article has described a model of stages or one stage of family therapy. This volume concentrates attention on the concepts and theoretical applications, provides practical illustrations, and examines the issues related to stages in the process of family therapy.

Family therapy is a complex process involving a therapist entering a family system to form a new temporary system with the intent of producing change in the family's functioning. Clearly, there is no standard set of stages the process follows. The therapist's theoretical orientation and methods, as well as the characteristics of the family and problems, influence the process. However, a therapist has goals and uses methods and techniques to progress toward the goals. An understanding of the stages in the process of family therapy can help the therapist place a single event in perspective and plan interventions rather than simply react to the situation. This volume will help therapists conceptualize therapy over stages rather than in terms of a single interview. It will also give practical examples from different theories and types of problems.

The editor of this volume is Douglas Breunlin. He is the Director of the Family Systems Program at the Institute for Juvenile Research in Chicago, a program that has been involved in an advanced level of training for fifteen years. He is also an adjunct faculty member in the University of Illinois School of Medicine. His professional interests involve pediatrics and family practice and he consults in both departments in Cook County Hospital. Mr. Breunlin has selected an outstanding group of authors. Each is a practicing family therapist who has presented stimulating ideas and examples that have implications for other practitioners.

James C. Hansen
Series Editor

Preface

To every thing there is a season, and a time to every purpose under heaven. . . .

Ecclesiastes 3:1

Prophets and wise men seem to understand that pattern and timing connect the events in our lives, circumscribing, for most processes, a beginning, middle, and end. Family therapy, too, may be viewed as a whole process connected by patterns and timing issues. In the family therapy literature, this process has generally been addressed as the stages of family therapy. The emphasis, however, has been on the demarcation of discrete stages, such as assessment, treatment, and termination, that occur in sequential order. Far less attention has been devoted to the subtle and complex temporal relationships that exist among the stages or component parts of family therapy.

This volume attempts to address this gap in the literature. It begins with a premise that the process of therapy as a whole can and should be described, understood, and considered when conducting therapy. The volume offers a perspective that removes therapists from a "one session at a time" mentality, and urges a stance in which each session is conducted with consideration for the preceding and subsequent sessions and the therapy as a whole.

Describing, understanding, and drawing useful guidelines from considerations of therapy as a whole are difficult because family therapy does not lend itself easily to this type of analysis. Therapy is a process that extends over an indefinite period of time, and is punctuated by intense one-hour sessions whose intervals are frequently long and irregular. Often it is not entirely clear why a therapy begins or why it ends, or, moreover, who is in charge of these decisions. As a whole, therapy is a rambling and loosely connected process wherein most of the action takes place outside the therapist's office. It is not surprising, therefore, that therapists prefer to describe that aspect of therapy which they see and, to some extent, control; that is, the sessions, themselves. It is far more difficult to describe the pattern that connects these sessions. Still, just as negative space is vital to a dance or a sculpture, the whole of therapy can only be fully described by the sessions, their relationship to each other, and the events surrounding them.

Grappling with the process of therapy as a whole within the context of an edited volume has proved to be very challenging. In the end, I decided against a series of articles in which each contributor describes one stage or component of this whole. Such an endeavor would replicate the current and somewhat narrow view of stages as sequential events. Rather, I have elected to approach the concepts of stages from three points of reference that, taken together, offer complementary views of this complex and subtle topic. The first point of reference is the process of therapy, itself. Included are articles that address the beginning, middle, and end of family therapy. The second point is that of a particular therapy model. Included are articles that discuss how strategic and structural family therapy conceptualize the therapy process in stages. The third vantage point is a characteristic of the family presenting for treatment. Two articles, one in which the family presents with a severely disturbed adolescent, and one in which the family is undergoing the process of divorce, are included. These articles illustrate how the stages of therapy must often accommodate the circumstances presented by the family. Finally, I also include two articles that attempt to connect the concept of stages closer to the mainstream of family therapy. Taken together, the nine articles afford the reader an opportunity to encounter the stages of family therapy and their relationship to one another in complementary ways, and, I hope, in ways that connect with the reader's own clinical work.

In the first article, I attempt a reformulation of the concept of therapy in stages by expanding upon the ideas introduced above. I also argue that the well-accepted systems concepts of ahistory, isomorphism, and discontinuity have contributed to a "one session at a time" approach to therapy, but can be expanded to include the concept of stages. Included also in this article is a review of the literature on stages. This review suggests that staging can be viewed from three levels:

1. the evolution of therapeutic relationships
2. the process of change
3. the technical and/or administrative aspects of therapy

Finally, I suggest the stages of family that emerge from the literature as a consensus.

In the next article Rocco Cimmarusti and Jay Lappin tackle the beginning of family therapy. These authors propose that a successful beginning requires a problem redefinition and that four tasks must receive attention simultaneously. The four tasks—engaging, assessing, setting goals, and initiating the process of change—and a problem redefinition can be achieved, in their view, through the creation of a workable reality. While the authors' preference for structural family therapy is apparent, the article serves as a useful blueprint for anyone to begin family therapy.

Next, Dennis McGuire accepts the challenge of defining and implementing the elusive middle phase of family therapy. McGuire suggests that this uncharted and frequently endless phase of therapy can be organized by paying particular attention to three variables: belief systems, structure, and developmental concerns. He defines each variable and describes how it can become a point of leverage during the middle phase and assist the therapist in avoiding stances that prolong therapy or result in premature termination.

In the article on ending family therapy Anthony Heath offers a novel and practical approach to termination. He argues that while most family therapists hold a concept of ideal termination, in practice, therapy rarely ends that way. He proposes that family therapists would do well to follow the medical practice model of termination. Heath cogently defines and explores the benefits of this model, and offers practical guidelines for its implementation. A useful dimension of this article is the connection Heath draws between therapist positions taken at the beginning of therapy and later issues surrounding termination.

Betty Karrer and John Schwartzman then examine the stages of Structural Family Therapy. These authors discuss the use of spatial and temporal dimensions in Structural Family Therapy and argue that staging must take into account both dimensions. This is accomplished when the therapist first creates a framework for change that defines the various holons and how they must change. The authors then illustrate how this framework for change serves as a blueprint for subsequent therapy sessions. Karrer and Schwartzman clearly demonstrate that even Structural Family Therapy, with its strong in-session focus, is amenable to conceptualization in stages.

Shifting vantage points, in the next article Judith Mazza describes the stages of Strategic Therapy. Expanding on Haley's (1976) seminal work on the stages of family therapy, Mazza argues that staging must be tailored for each case. The stages of a specific therapy, she notes, may follow stages similar to those which the family experienced leading up to the problem, but in the reverse order. She also defines key variables of therapy that mark particular stages of therapy, including the problem, directives, therapist involvement, rapport, strategies, and unit of treatment. In a case study, she illustrates the creative manner in which a strategic therapist can use the concept of stages.

Virginia Simons then examines the stages of therapy for families going through the process of divorce. First, she summarizes the process of separation and divorce and the changes in family structure that accompany this process. She then describes a two-stage treatment model that follows the family through separation and divorce. The first stage addresses therapeutic concerns during the dissolution of the marriage. The second stage addresses therapeutic concerns through the recovery after the divorce and includes three phases: differentiation, reintegration, and readjustment. The need for the therapist to attend carefully to issues of timing is evident throughout this article.

Once again shifting vantage points, Susan Mackey· discusses the stages of family therapy with severely disturbed adolescents. She proposes that success with these cases is frequently contingent upon a careful staging of the therapy process. Her seven-stage model is embedded within a set of six pragmatic guidelines that, together with the stages, offer a therapist a pragmatic and flexible approach for treating these families. A particular asset of the model is the careful consideration given to timing issues that orchestrate events involving the broader context of the family with those taking place in the sessions.

Finally, Richard Schwartz offers a meta-view of the stages, themselves, and asks whether family therapy has reached the stage where it can appreciate the concept of stages. He traces the evolution of the field of family therapy, the models of family therapy, and individual therapists through three stages: an essentialistic stage, a transitional stage, and a relativity stage. He proposes that the subtleties of the staging process are most easily recognized and implemented in the relativity stage. Schwartz argues that family therapy, with its many models, is now moving beyond the essentialistic stage, in which each model developed specific techniques to cure what was believed to be the essence of human problems, to a relativistic stage where the language of flexibility, timing, context, and relationship to other techniques and concepts is fast replacing the dogma, arrogance, and fervor with which family therapists used to speak. The answer to his question, he believes, is yes.

This volume is not intended to be an exhaustive exposition of the concept of stages. Indeed, it cannot be because there remains much that we do not understand about the patterns and timing that effectively create a process of change. Hopefully, it will challenge the reader to sit back and question the relationships between the events we call therapy and to recognize more fully that "to every thing there is a season."

Douglas C. Breunlin
Volume Editor

REFERENCE

Haley, J. *Problem solving therapy*. New York: Harper Colophon, 1976.

Acknowledgments

I would like to thank John Steffek, M.D., the Director of the Institute for Juvenile Research, for his strong support for writing undertaken within the Family Systems Program; Nikki Holloway and Joann Godbold for their excellent secretarial assistance; and the faculty and students of the Family Systems Program for their many helpful suggestions.

1. Expanding the Concept of Stages in Family Therapy

Douglas C. Breunlin

I awoke with a start. We had overslept. Pandemonium followed; no clothes had been laid out for the kids, coffee readied, or homework checked. The kids reacted and we blamed them for not cooperating. I was already late, so I made a move to leave for work.

"Don't forget to take the chair so you can buy stain for it," called my wife as I was halfway out the door.

It was cold. The car hesitated and, like me, reluctantly came to life. Impatient, I pulled out of the garage, but the car died. I cursed, and fiddled with the radio while the car warmed up. The newscaster was discussing the latest attempts at arms control negotiation with an expert on Soviet affairs.

"What effect did Reagan's meeting with Gromyko have on the prospect for talks?" he asked.

"I believe it's a first step. It sends a clear message to the Soviets that the White House is ready to talk," replied the expert.

I hit another station and got a review of Sunday's football game: "Chicago's failure to establish an inside running attack early in the game enabled San Diego to blitz more often. This effectively defensed Chicago's passing, and when Chicago fell behind, the pass was not an effective weapon to score quickly."

"They do it every week," I thought. "Doesn't the coach ever listen to the news?"

I stopped at a hardware store. Chair in hand I entered, and looked for the owner, knowing he would most likely possess the knowledge I needed.

"I'd like to buy some stain for this chair," I told him.

"Let's have a closer look," he said. He fondled the chair as if it were a child. "Can I give you a little advice?" he asked.

"Please. You're talking to someone who's never done anything like this before."

"Well, first, it's nowhere near ready for stain yet. See, it still needs more sanding. Once you get it sanded proper you'll be able to tell whether it needs a filler. Then you have a choice of stains, or maybe a clear finish would be enough."

"It could take a long time to finish this chair," I complained, hoping he would disagree.

"If you want it to look decent, you have to go at it the right way," he said.

When I arrived at work, a student was waiting for me.

"Mrs. Jones called. She says her son is worse. But the school says he's better, and even father says so. She wants to come in today. Should we see her?"

We discussed the pros and cons of a session, finally deciding not to risk the progress we had made by putting her off. I agreed to supervise the session, realizing as I did so that a morning set aside for writing had just vanished.

Later in the day I headed for the library and began my usual warm-up routine for a paper: free associating about the topic and writing disconnected thoughts on paper. "Why is it," I mused, "that therapists seem to dislike thinking in terms of stages?" I jotted down the words *discontinuity, isomorphism, ahistory, pragmatism,* and *cookbook.* Several ideas later, with a growing anxiety that these scribblings had to be translated into a publishable paper, I yawned, put my head down, dozed off, and began to dream.

The President and a Soviet diplomat were embroiled in an argument. They were perched on large chairs and wore football helmets with missiles attached to them. The Soviet diplomat was bouncing in his chair and screaming, "If Mr. Breunlin does not submit an adequate document on stages, there will be no talks."

"It will take time," replied the President.

Unsatisfied, the diplomat bounced even higher until a loud cracking sound was heard and the chair fell to pieces, leaving the diplomat sprawled on the floor. Livid, he raised himself to his knees.

"Adequate chairs, that was the one inviolable condition of our talks!"

His eyes pierced the president, who looked on in horror as the diplomat groped for the button on his helmet.

I awoke with a start, perspiration on my back. There must be something about stages, I thought, as I headed to my car and debated whether to call home to say I'd be late for supper.

Virtually every aspect of life involves a process that begins and ends. Whether it concerns a morning routine, a home project, an athletic contest, an international negotiation session, or a research paper, the process unfolds in stages. Sometimes the stages are obvious; at other times, however, they are extremely subtle and not readily detected. In the pursuit of a process, it is easy to overlook these stages. The consequences can be failure, chaos, and loss of control, as in the dream described above.

Even in the final product of a process, the complexity of the stages in its creation can be appreciated. In a gallery, for example, the connoisseur of art knows that hundreds of sketches preceded the final decision about the subject of an oil painting. Beneath the dazzling beauty of the oil are the penciled circles and squares that block out the figures and the receding lines that define perspective. Over these lines lies the paint initially applied, long since rejected and covered over as the artist struggled with issues of light, texture, and unity. The talent and patience of the artist are buried beneath the silent and final statement of the painting itself.

Therapy, too, is a process with a beginning, a middle, and an end—with stages. Surprisingly, many family therapists behave as if therapy has no stages. In fact, the concept of therapy in stages does not occupy a central position within the field of family therapy. Since 1976, when Jay Haley first wrote about therapy in stages, a bit more attention has been devoted to the concept. A literature review produced 46 articles in which stages of therapy are discussed, but, still, this is a mere fraction of the family therapy literature.

This volume focuses on the stages of family therapy. For it to be taken seriously, the concept of stages, itself, must be shown to have relevance for family therapists. This article attempts to increase the relevance of the concept of stages by expanding its meaning beyond that currently used in the literature, and by reconciling it with three major and discordant family therapy concepts; ahistory, isomorphism, and discontinuity. I will also summarize the literature on stages, and suggest six stages that emerge as a consensus from it.

EXPANDING THE MEANING OF STAGES

Therapists' rejection of the concept of stages may be derived partially from guilt by association. Hoffman (1981) noted that Haleys' main work on stages, *Problem Solving Therapy* (1978), represented "a strange leap, from one side of Bateson's zigzag to the other, from process to form" (p. 280). Because of its emphasis on form, Haley's concept of stages became associated primarily with a pragmatic approach to therapy that was designed to interrupt behavioral sequences and their structures. In *Leaving Home* (1980), Haley moved even further in this direction, cautioning against the use of process language (e.g., metaphors and analogies) and recommending the safer, albeit simpler, digital communication. Hence, the concept of stages became linked to a largely behavioral, pragmatic, digital, and problem-focused type of therapy.

Other models of family therapy that explicitly included stages of therapy, such as the McMaster model (Epstein & Bishop, 1981) and the functional family therapy model (Alexander, Barton, Waldron, & Mas, 1983), also associated the concept of stages and a pragmatic, behavioral style of therapy with a "the therapist will fix it" mentality toward human dilemmas. As a result, these models and stages are often attacked for their naivete and simplicity. Epstein and Bishop (1981) claimed that such accusations are unwarranted. They argued that stages are essential if one is to operationalize a therapy and make it accessible to research. They also contended that stages are vital guideposts for beginners and provide a useful infrastructure for experienced therapists.

The points made by Epstein and Bishop (1981) apply to all models of therapy, not just those that are pragmatic, problem-focused, and behavioral. Even so, family therapy is more than a series of easily identified steps designated by a therapist and followed conveniently by a family. While few would disagree that, to conduct family therapy, it is necessary to engage in activities such as assessing, setting goals, intervening and terminating, the process as a whole is by far more complex. Were it not, family therapy would by now have emerged as a more predictable endeavor.

To articulate accurately how the process of family therapy is staged, one needs a more flexible and complex definition of staging. Music offers a useful analogy to describe the difference between simple descriptions of stages and the expanded description I believe is essential if staging is to be relevant. Using just the notes, one can play a melody that constitutes music of sorts. One can even play a song by repeating the melody for all of the stanzas. But anyone who has listened to a child practice knows there is more to music than the melody. This becomes even more evident upon examination of sheet music. To be sure, a central part of sheet music is the notes that create the melody. But the melody is played in a key and a defined tempo and both may change at some point in the musical score. Moreover, the volume and intensity of the music are defined by crescendos, and the notes may also be prolonged or softened. If the musical score is lengthy, it may be broken into movements, with each movement bearing a relationship to the others and to the whole. Leitmotifs may also be used to introduce recurrent themes that further tie the piece together. If one adds orchestration, then the complex interplay of many instruments becomes possible.

The sheet music provides the structure through which the many components of music bear relationship to one another. Together the components define a process that becomes a whole, the music. Listening to and watching a symphony, one marvels at the ease with which the expert conductor brings unity and meaning to the music, but, again, one need only watch an amateur conductor to appreciate the complexity of the process.

In its most simple form, therapy in stages is analogous to making music by playing the melody—necessary, but not sufficient to convey the process fully. Assessing, setting goals, treating, and terminating are like the melody—necessary but not sufficient to fully define the therapy. At its most complex, therapy in stages is analogous to a concert performance of a Beethoven symphony. The creativity of the conductor finds an outlet in the complexity of the musical score. The stages of therapy are comparable to the structure of the music. As in music, timing and intensity can be varied in therapy. There are movements, sometimes lasting for several sessions, and leitmotifs or recurrent themes woven through the therapy. A skilled therapist knows that the process of therapy will reveal interrelated components that can be used to unify the therapy and give it direction. There remains great latitude for creativity and diversity among therapists within the structure provided by the stages, just as there are opportunities for several conductors to make very different interpretations of the same musical score.

Many therapists accept this expanded view of stages, but do not apply it to their work. This discrepancy between belief and practice may result, in part, from the timing of therapy. Unlike music, in which movements bear an immediate relationship to one another, therapy is generally a series of sessions punctuated by relatively long gaps of time. Thus, therapists may approach each session as if it were "the therapy," rather than just a part of therapy. Furthermore, family therapy, even more than other types of therapy, includes certain concepts that militate against thinking in terms of stages: ahistory, isomorphism, and discontinuity. The expanded meaning of therapy in stages must be reconciled with these concepts before it can be completely accepted.

Ahistory

In the 1960s, it became fashionable for therapists to describe themselves as "working in the here and now." This cliche was granted theoretical credibility by systems theory and cybernetics, in both of which behavior was purported to be maintained by the current functioning of a system. Thus it was easy to abolish the past, and through a similar, but less justified, sleight of hand, the future. Just because one believes that the past did not cause the present, it does not follow that the present will not influence the future; if it did not, change would never occur. Furthermore, the ability to predict the effect of present actions on the future is a sine qua non of success in endeavors of all sorts, from athletics to politics, marketing, parenting, and even therapy. The essence of stages in therapy is that there is a close fit between action in the present and subsequent events.

History is slowly creeping back into the family therapy field. With such terms as presenting edge, onset of problem, and partial arc, it is again becoming possible to ground behavior in the context of time. Therapists should recognize that the presenting phenomena of any given session are, in part, a function of the therapy preceding it. Once again, stages become relevant; present procedure is in part defined and limited by previous events.

Isomorphism

The emphasis on the present (and the consequent deemphasis on stages) is intensified in the concept of isomorphism. Literally meaning same structure, the term *isomorphism* suggests that the interaction of a family in a therapy session not only reveals necessary information about the family, but also provides the essential ingredients for change in the family. Isomorphism taken to its extreme represents a sort of family transference; the family is bound to present its structure, regardless of the context of therapy. Stated in this way, isomorphism becomes acontextual and atemporal, thus violating one of the fundamental axioms of systems theory—that behavior is a function of context.

A family does present its structure in therapy, but the structure will exhibit interactions that are a function of the context of therapy. When a mother defends her son's behavior to a therapist, for example, the isomorphism of that interaction in the first session may well differ from that of the same interaction in the fifth session. In the first session, the interaction is isomorphic to how the family is structured when it encounters a threatening and novel situation (therapy) conducted by an unfamiliar individual (a therapist) whose age, sex, and style are also a part of that context. To evoke isomorphism and conclude that the interaction indicates an overprotective mother is to ignore the context in which the interaction occurs.

The expanded meaning of stages suggests that a family's presentation in therapy depends in part on the time of that presentation. Hence, a family may become dysfunctional at various points in the therapy, but for different reasons: to convince the therapist of the family's need for help, to deal with fear of the unknown, or to postpone the termination of therapy. A therapist's response to each act is contingent on the context in which it occurs, that is, the specific stage of the therapy process.

The here-and-now interactions observable in any session also do not provide all the information needed to assess the total structure or pattern of a family (Breunlin & Schwartz, in press). The short sequences that can be seen in a session are embedded in a series of interlocking sequences of longer duration. These longer sequences may have a period or cycle of one day and reflect a family's routine, while others have periods ranging from a month to a year. Examples of longer sequences are recurrent hospitalizations and periodic oscillations in the level of intimacy between a couple. The micro-transactions observed in a session, therefore, while isomorphic with the total pattern, are not the total pattern. Moreover, before change can occur, it may be necessary to address sequences of longer duration. This view forces a therapist to look for and attempt to change sequences in which the cycle spans several sessions.

Discontinuity

Hoffman (1981) argued that families change through sudden transformations in which new and more functional behavior abruptly appears. This discontinuity theory blurs the issues of the timing of change and, hence, renders the concept of stages irrelevant. Liddle and Saba (1983) very clearly addressed this issue:

> Another dimension is the factor, or the definition of when change can be said to occur. A discontinuous only description creates the illusion of specificity (Whitehead's fallacy of misplaced concreteness) regarding

the timing of change. How is it possible to be so sure that change has occurred precisely at the (apparent) leap of transformation? Such leaps are compelling, dramatic descriptors, but they are weak on explanatory substance. Some physicists were equally convinced of the particle aspects of subatomic matter until their colleagues saw the identical reality in a different way—as a wave of process. A discontinuous interpretation of change encourages snapshot-like slices of what, from other perspectives, would be seen as process versions of reality. The concept of time is therefore crucial here from the point of view considering when the assessment (and punctuation) of change occurs. A discontinuous paradigm shines the spotlight of change evaluation only onto noticeable changes. Outside this ring of illumination, however, are less clearly discernible aspects of the change in question. In these shadows may lurk the precursors and consequences of transformation, perhaps vital components of an advanced understanding of the process and context of human change. (p. 168)

Unfortunately, authors on family therapy contribute to confusion about change by highlighting the dramatic moments, those in which the big leap of change appears to have occurred, in their clinical examples. Interestingly, such moments often occur well into therapy (10 or more sessions). Moreover, when the leap occurs in the first session or early in the therapy, the precursors may have been initiated in another context (e.g., school community, relatives) before the start of therapy. The process leading up to the change is almost never examined, however, even though change may never have occurred without this process.

A close examination of the entire process of therapy reveals that the context for change is, indeed, more than a sudden moment. Consequently, even when therapists accept the assumption of discontinuous change, they do so with an awareness that sessions in which no change occurs bear a significant relationship to that one session in which the big leap is made.

If one allows then for a rethinking of history, isomorphism, and discontinuity, I believe the expanded view of stages becomes applicable to all models of therapy— not just those emphasizing the digital, behavior- and problem-focused elements of therapy. The challenge is to articulate a framework of stages that is relevant yet flexible enough to be useful to a creative therapist.

THE STAGES OF FAMILY THERAPY

What are the stages of family therapy? Perusing the family therapy literature, it becomes obvious that the answer depends in large measure upon the perspective of the observer describing the therapy. Little information about stages can be gathered from articles that use a theoretical concept (e.g., boundary) or an intervention (e.g., creation of intensity) as the organizing metaphor for the therapy. Such articles make it appear that concepts and interventions apply at any point in the process of therapy. The more the observer's lens is narrowed, however, the more likely it is that therapy can be described in terms of stages.

Of those authors who have developed a general model of family therapy, only Freeman (1976, 1977), Shilling and Gross (1979), and Solomon (1977) have attempted an explanation of stages (Table 1–1). If the lens is narrowed and a specific model described, the number of references to stages increases, but not dramatically. Nine such models, some well known, others less so, are also included in Table 1–1. When the lens is narrowed even further to focus on the process of therapy with a particular kind of case, stages are more readily explicated. The focus may involve a particular problem (e.g., alcoholism, child abuse), population (e.g., those in interracial marriages, Vietnamese), or family process (e.g., divorce, mourning). Studies of a particular problem or population reveal redundancies in the therapy that can be translated into stages. Studies of family processes show that therapy must be synchronized with a family process if therapy is to be successful. Finally, there are numerous examples of single case studies in which stages are described. Sources are indicated in Table 1–2.

If the stages cited in these tables were combined, the result would prove bewildering. In writing about stages, each author is selective regarding the specification of stages, highlighting that which is central to the model and taking for granted or ignoring that which is not deemed crucial. Some common denominators begin to emerge, however. The selectivity generally produces three levels of staging:

1. staging with regard to the process of change
2. staging with regard to the development, maintenance, and termination of therapeutic relationships
3. staging with regard to the technical and/or administrative aspects of therapy

To the extent that authors consider a level of staging crucial to therapy, they clearly define specific stages within that level. For example, Haley (1976) organized stages primarily around the process of change. In describing the stages of a case, he noted, "In the approach to be described here only the key moves in the therapy [those that produce change] are emphasized" (p. 131). Although Haley took the work on relationships and administrative issues for granted, it should not be assumed that he considered them unimportant.

Other authors proposed that change takes place primarily through the therapeutic relationship. They are more likely to emphasize the forming, maintaining, and ending of relationships, including stages that take into account the problematic changes that occur in relationships throughout the course of therapy (Bell, 1977; Powell & Gazda, 1979).

Table 1–1 Stages of Family Therapy Presented in the Literature

Author(s)	Model	No. of Stages	Stages
Freeman (1976, 1977)	Family therapy	3	1. Problem redefinitions 2. Recognition of need to work together 3. Termination
Schilling & Gross (1979)	Family therapy	4	1. Preparation 2. Transition 3. Consolidation 4. Termination
Solomon (1977)	Family therapy	5	1. Deal with anxiety about treatment 2. Relinquish labeling and identify generalized discomfort 3. Explore complementarity of family discomfort 4. Plan changes in the problem-solving mechanism of the family system 5. Relinquish the therapist
Haley (1976)	Strategic therapy	4	1. First interview: social stage, problem stage, interaction stage, and definition of desired changes 2. Creation of an abnormal organization to shift the problem 3. Focus on parents and blocking of problem return 4. Disengagement
Alexander, Barton, Waldron, & Mas (1983)	Functional family therapy	5	1. Introduction-impression 2. Assessment-understanding 3. Induction-therapy 4. Treatment-education 5. Generalization-termination
Breunlin (1983)	Structural-strategic	4	1. Engage 2. Establish an abnormal stage to unbalance the family 3. Deal with the consequences of change

Table 1–1 continued

Author(s)	Model	No. of Stages	Stages
			4. Normalize family functioning and disengage from the family
Kantor (1983)	Structural-analytic	3	1. Problem relief 2. Transformation of the disabled structure underlying system disablement 3. Prevention of future disablement by involving next most vulnerable structure
Epstein & Bishop (1981)	Problem-centered systems therapy	4	1. Assessing 2. Contracting 3. Treating 4. Closing
Powell & Gazda (1979)	Adlerian family therapy	4	1. Establishment of rapport 2. Assessment 3. Interpretation 4. Reorientation
Schneider, Schonitzer, & Friedricks (1981)	Graphic family therapy	4	1. Analysis 2. Motivation 3. Evaluation 4. Research
Bell (1977)	Group family therapy	7	1. Initiation 2. Testing 3. Struggle for power 4. Settling on a common task 5. Struggles toward completion 6. Completion 7. Separation from therapy
Vass, Jacobs, & Slavek	Live-in family counseling	6	1. Entrance into the flow of family routine 2. Intervention in family routine 3. Conversation with individual family members 4. Group processing 5. Establishment of self-monitoring program 6. Follow-up

Table 1–2 Surveying the Literature for Stages

Focus on Family Process

Author(s)	Process	Author(s)	Process
Sluzki (1979)	Migration	Vore & Wright (1974)	Dying
Lappin (1983)	Migration	Carey (1977)	Death
Bardene, Hill, & Serritella (1978)	Divorce	Gelcer (1983)	Mourning
Storm & Sprenkle (1982)	Divorce	Cantor (1975)	Suicide, effects of
Hancock (1980)	Divorce	Gross (1975)	Foster placement
Fine (1980)	Custody	Random, Schlesinger, & Derdyn (1979)	Step-family, formation
Cleveland & Irwin (1982)	Custody	Landau & Griffiths (1981)	South African family, transition
Woody (1983)	Sexuality in divorce	Combrinck-Graham, Gursky, & Brendler (1982)	Hospitalization

Focus on Problem

Author(s)	Problem
Guttman (1973)	Psychosis
Usher, Jeffrey, & Glass (1982)	Alcoholism
Foley (1976)	Alcoholism
Bray (1978)	Spinal cord
Sandler (1977)	Asthma
Huberty & Huberty (1976)	Drug abuse
Mueller & Orfanidis (1976)	Schizophrenia
Wolkenstein (1977)	Child abuse

Focus on Populations

Author(s)	Population
Jurich (1983)	Vietnam veterans
Faulkner & Kich (1983)	Interracial family
Zinner (1978)	Borderline adolescents
Sakamoto (1976)	Psychotics, Japanese
Chabot (1976)	Acting out male

Finally, in many cases, it appears that the success of therapy is contingent on careful staging of the administrative aspects of the therapy. These administrative aspects are of two types: (1) decisions that the therapist makes in preparation for subsequent interactions with the family and (2) orchestration of the larger context in which the case is embedded. The first includes decisions about who should be invited to sessions, which problems should be given special attention, now sessions should be spaced, and how between-session contacts and breaks in therapy should be managed. The second involves the legwork and strategic interventions with larger systems that influence the course of therapy, such as making contacts with school personnel, legal and social institutions, and other mental health professionals whose expertise may be needed in the case.

Although an awareness that staging occurs at three levels helps to eliminate confusion, it is still not possible simply to make three lists of stages that cover all models. First, the levels are not mutually exclusive; for example, the way in which a family forms a relationship with a therapist also provides vital clues for assessment. Second, the stages are often juxtaposed differently in different models. Finally, the timing and the closure of stages vary across models. With the structural and strategic models, for example, therapists are content to attempt change based on a partial assessment of family functioning; with other models, therapists prefer a more thorough assessment before attempting interventions.

Stages That Emerge from the Literature

The following stages of family therapy appear to emerge as a consensus from the literature:

1. beginning. The therapist must organize the context of therapy (referrer and other systems), convene the family (selection of unit), initiate therapeutic relationships, assess family relationships, and clarify the problem.
2. redefining the problem. The therapist must redefine the problem in interactional and solvable terms, establish goals, ensure that all interested parties agree on goals, solidify relationships, and confirm the necessary treatment unit.
3. attempting change initially. Within the framework of a preferred model, the therapist must select interventions that make a small but significant change, read the feedback from these interventions, ensure that all interested parties recognize change, and monitor resistance to change.
4. consolidating and dealing with the consequences of change. The therapist must intervene to seal the change, read feedback for negative consequences of change and deal with any such consequences, evaluate developmental deficits and undertake any necessary interventions, and shift to other problem areas if necessary.

5. ending. The therapist must predict the duration of therapy, normalize functioning, create a graceful exit, and allow for family return, if necessary.

These stages are not exhaustive, nor do they convey all the subtleties of the therapeutic process. Rather, they indicate the structure of the therapeutic process as a whole. Stages are like a musical score; they provide a structure within which the therapist is free to be creative.

Failure to follow the stages or omission of some stages does not automatically result in failure. In some cases, particularly those that are straightforward, stages can be skipped with impunity. In other cases, a staging error presents difficulties that can only be solved by incorporating the incomplete or missed stage. When the therapist repeatedly fails to read the feedback and forces the family to respond to the wrong stage, however, therapy is likely to fail.

In closing, I offer one final metaphor. A therapist is like a pole vaulter, one of the most versatile of all professionals. The pole vaulter possesses a blend of exquisite skills: speed, strength, endurance, agility, timing, and courage. The fluency of the performance defies analysis, and hides the precise stages involved. Hidden are the careful measuring of steps, the wait for a tail wind, the correct placement of the hands, the mental preparation and, yes, the selection of the pole. We see only a fluid process, but the pole vaulter, reviewing frame-by-frame a movie of a missed vault, could detect the moment of error. He might say: "I didn't develop enough speed on the runway, the planting of the pole or my transition came too late, I pushed off too soon, my follow through was stiff," or "my heart just wasn't in it."

REFERENCES

Alexander, J., Barton, C., Waldron, H., & Mas, H. (1983). Beyond the technology of family therapy: The anatomy of intervention model. In K.D. Craig & R. McMahon (Eds.), *Advances in clinical behavior therapy*. New York: Brunner/Mazel.

Baideme, S.M., Hill, H.A., & Serritella, D.A. (1978). Conjoint family therapy following divorce: An alternative strategy. *American Journal of Family Therapy, 6*(1), 55–59.

Bell, J.E. (1977). Family in medical and psychiatric treatment: Selected clinical approaches. *Journal of Operational Psychiatry, 8*(1), 57–65.

Bray, G.P. (1978). Rehabilitation of spinal cord injured: A family approach. *Journal of Applied Rehabilitation Counseling, 9*(3), 70–78.

Breunlin, D.C. (1983). Therapy in stages: A life cycle view. In H.A. Liddle (Ed.), *Family therapy collections: Vol. 7. Clinical implications of the family life cycle* (pp. 1–11). Rockville, Md.: Aspen Systems Corporation.

Breunlin, D.C., & Schwartz, R.C. Sequences toward a common denominator for family therapy. Manuscript submitted for publication.

Cantor, P. (1975). The effects of youthful suicide on the family. *Psychiatric Opinion, 12*(6), 6–11.

Carey, A. (1977). Helping the child and the family cope with death. *American Journal of Family Therapy, 5*(1), 58–63.

Chabot, D.R. (1976). Family therapy with court-committed, institutionalized, acting-out, male adolescents. *Clinical Psychologist, 29*(4), 8–9.

Cleveland, M., & Irvin, K. (1982). Custody resolution counseling: An alternative intervention *Journal of Marital and Family Therapy, 8*(1), 105–111.

Combrinck-Graham, L., Gursky, E.J., & Brendler, J. (1982). Hospitalization of single-parent families of disturbed children. *Family Process, 21*(2), 141–152.

Epstein, N.B., & Bishop, D.S. (1981). Problem centered systems therapy of the family. *Journal of Marital & Family Therapy, 7*(1), 23–31.

Faulkner, J., & Kich, G.K. (1983). Assessment and engagement in therapy with the interracial family. In C. Falicov (Ed.), *Cultural Perspectives in Family Therapy.* In *Family therapy collections,* (6) 78–90. Rockville, Md.: Aspen Systems Corporation.

Fine, S. (1980). Children in divorce, custody and access situations: The contribution of the mental health professional. *Journal of Child Psychology & Psychiatry & Allied Disciplines, 21*(4), 353–361.

Foley, V.D. (1976). Alcoholism: A family system approach. *Journal of Family Counseling, 4*(2), 12–18.

Freeman, D.S. (1976). Phases of family treatment. *Family Coordinator, 25*(3), 265–270.

Freeman, D.S. (1977). The use of time in family therapy. *Family Therapy, 4*(3), 195–206.

Gelcer, E. (1983). Mourning is a family affair. *Family Process, 22*(4), 501–516.

Gross, G. (1975). Foster home placements: Conjoint family therapy for the foster family's role dilemma. *Family Therapy, 2*(1), 57–61.

Guttman, H.A. (1973). A contraindication for family therapy: The prepsychotic or postpsychotic young adult and his parents. *Archives of General Psychiatry, 29*(3), 352–355.

Haley, J. (1978). *Problem solving therapy.* New York: Harper Colophon.

Haley, J. (1980). *Leaving home.* New York: McGraw-Hill.

Hancock, E. (1980). The dimensions of meaning and belonging in the process of divorce. *American Journal of Orthopsychiatry, 50*(1), 18–27.

Hoffman, L. (1981). *Foundations of family therapy.* New York: Basic Books.

Huberty, C.E., & Huberty, D.J. (1976). Treating the parents of adolescent drug abusers. *Contemporary Drug Problems, 5*(4), 573–592.

Jurich, A.P. (1983). The Saigon of the family's mind: Family therapy with families of Vietnam veterans. *Journal of Marital and Family Therapy, 9*(4), 355–363.

Kantor, D. (1983). The structural-analytic approach to the treatment of family developmental crisis. In H.A. Liddle (Ed.), *Family therapy collections: Clinical implications of the family life cycle,* (7) 12–34. Rockville, Md.: Aspen Systems Corporation.

Landau, J., & Griffiths, J. (1981). The South African family in transition: Training and therapeutic implications. *Journal of Marital & Family Therapy, 7*(3), 339–344.

Lappin, J. (1983). On becoming a culturally conscious family therapist. In C. Falicov (Ed.), *Family therapy collections, Cultural perspectives in family therapy* (6) 122–136. Rockville, Md.: Aspen Systems Corporation.

Liddle, H.A., & Saba, G. (1983). Clinical use of the family life cycle: Some cautionary guidelines. In H.A. Liddle (Ed.), *Family therapy collections: Clinical implications of the family life cycle* (7) 161–172. Rockville, Md.: Aspen Systems Corporation.

Mueller, P.S., & Orfanidis, M.M. (1976). A method of co-therapy for schizophrenic families. *Family Process, 15*(2), 179–191.

Powell, G.S., & Gazda, G.M. (1979). "Cleaning out the trash": A case study in Adlerian family counseling. *Journal of Individual Psychology, 35*(1), 45–57.

Ransom, J.W., Schlesinger, S., & Derdeyn, A.P. (1979). A stepfamily in formation. *American Journal of Orthopsychiatry, 49*(1), 36–43.

Sakamota, Y. (1976–1977). Some experiences through family-psychotherapy for psychotics in Japan. *International Journal of Social Psychiatry, 22*(4), 265–271.

Sandler, N. (1977). Working with families of chronic asthmatics. *Journal of Asthma Research, 15*(1), 15–21.

Schilling, S.M., & Gross, E. (1979). Stages of family therapy: A developmental model. *Clinical Social Work Journal, 7*(2), 105–114.

Schneider, T., Schonitzer, D.L., & Friedricks, S. (1981). Graphic family therapy: An affective alternative to structure and strategy. *Journal of Marital & Family Therapy, 7*(1), 33–42.

Schwartz, R.C., Barret, M.J., & Saba, G. (1984). Bulimia for family therapy. In D. Garner & P. Garfinkel (Eds.), *Handbook for the treatment of anorexia nervosa and bulimia* (pp. 280–307). New York: Guilford.

Sluzki, C. (1979). Migration and family conflict. *Family Process, 18*, 379–390.

Solomon, M.A. (1977). The staging of family treatment: An approach to developing the therapeutic alliance. *Journal of Marriage & Family Counseling, 3*(2), 59–66.

Storm, C.L., & Sprenkle, D.H. (1982). Individual treatment in divorce therapy: A critique of an assumption. *Journal of Divorce, 6*(1–2), 87–97.

Usher, M.L., Jay, J., & Glass, D.R. (1982). Family therapy as a treatment modality for alcoholism. *Journal of Studies on Alcohol, 43*(9), 927–938.

Vass, M., Jacobs, E., & Slavek, N. (1984). Live-in family counseling: An integrated approach. *Personnel & Guidance Journal, 62*(7), 429–431.

Vore, D.A., & Wright, L. (1974). Psychological management of the family and the dying child. In R.E. Hardy & J.G. Cull (Eds.), *Therapeutic needs of the family: Problems, descriptions and therapeutic approaches* (pp. 125–147). Springfield, Ill.: Charles C Thomas.

Wolkenstein, A.S. (1977). The fear of committing child abuse: A discussion of eight families. *Child Welfare, 56*(4), 249–257.

Woody, J.D. (1983). Sexuality in divorce and remarriage. In J.D. Woody & R.H. Woody (Eds.), *Family therapy collections: Sexual issues in family therapy* (5), 62–81. Rockville, Md.: Aspen Systems Corporation.

Zinner, J. (1978). Combined individual and family therapy of borderline adolescents: Rationale and management of the early phase. *Adolescent Psychiatry, 6*, 420–427.

2. Beginning Family Therapy

Rocco A. Cimmarusti and Jay Lappin

If we are to serve the men and women who come to us for consultation, it is necessary to recognize the needs of each case and to cultivate an approach that will win confidence and cooperation.

Sidney E. Goldstein, 1945

We believe that the beginning stage of family therapy is a dynamic, complex process. It involves an interplay among the family, the therapist, and the broader context containing both. Thus, interventions that can manage this process and allow the therapist to do more than one thing at a time are most useful. Ideally, these interventions are dynamic and complex in their own right.

Other authors have struggled with the complex process of the beginning stage of family therapy and have provided valuable maps of the territory (Haley, 1976; Satir, 1964; Weakland, Fisch, Watzlawick & Bodin, 1974). These maps have given many family therapists a sense of security as they began the challenging process of working with families. In this article, our map offers the family therapist a panoramic view of the territory.

A useful start is to understand that the beginning stage of family therapy has tasks and a goal (Breunlin & Cimmarusti, 1983). The tasks are to engage the family, assess the problem, set goals, and initiate the process of change. The goal is to redefine the problem, thus offering new solutions to old problems. The various models of family therapy provide different ways to accomplish the goal of problem redefinition. Reframing, a technique for changing perspective of a problem—for example, calling a child "sad" instead of "bad"—is the vehicle for achieving this goal in one model (Watzlawick, Weakland, & Fisch, 1974). Another model utilizes positive connotation for the same purpose—attributing positive reasons to child's negative symptom. For example, the therapist may say an anorectic child is "sacrificing herself" for the good of the family (Selvini-Palazzoli, Boscolo, Cecchin, & Prata, 1978).

The creation of workable realities (Minuchin & Fishman, 1981) may or may not involve elements of reframing and positive connotation. The structural therapist,

16

depending on the idiosyncratic aspects of the context, might decide that it is more useful to intensify a negative label, for example choosing to "frame" a mildly bad little boy as a prospect for teenage delinquency, thus motivating a reluctant mother to take charge. A skilled therapist who constructs a workable reality not only accomplishes the tasks of the stage, but also arrives at a redefinition of the problem that arises from the completed tasks, rather than from some construction forced on the family. In order to construct such new realities, the therapist is joined with the family. In joining, the therapist adapts and challenges, leads and follows, is inducted in and distances from the family system.

Joining is not over when the problem has been redefined. It is an ongoing part of therapy. The dynamic interplay of joining and constructing a workable reality, in itself, initiates the process of change in the family. Thus, every action of the therapist attempts to promote change. The beginning stage of family therapy ends when a problem has been redefined and the redefinition has been accepted by the family. This, however, is not always possible at the end of the first session. When circumstances militate against a rapid problem redefinition, joining keeps the family returning until a workable reality is established.

The process of achieving the tasks and goals of the beginning stage of family therapy is not a direct progression. In fact, it is much like the process of climbing a mountain.* The climber does not simply go from the bottom to the top, but first must consider what equipment and provisions to take on the trip, what contingencies to plan for, and which route up the mountain to follow. The clinician, too, prepares for the "climb" through the beginning stage. Out-of-session issues, such as dealing with referral agents, working with collateral service providers, or drawing hypotheses about the family, and in-session issues, such as joining, assessing the problem, or reading feedback from the family, receive comparable consideration and planning.

Once the climbing party is well stocked and plans confirmed, the movement up the mountain begins. Basecamps, each one higher up the mountain than the previous one, are established to offer the climbers shelter and security from which to continue the climb. Without basecamps, a setback would require the climbers to return to the base of the mountain, and the goal of reaching the top might never be accomplished

The dynamic interplay of variables occurs both in and out of sessions. Working with the family's other service providers (e.g., teachers, school counselors, child welfare workers, probation officers) is an important part of the beginning stage of family therapy, because it affords the therapist more in-session freedom to concentrate on therapy per se with the family. The skills of joining and creating workable realities are as useful with other service providers as they are with

---

*We thank Richard C. Schwartz for passing on the mountain climbing metaphor, from Carlos Sluzksi.

families. Therapists' failure to use their skills with these other professionals, who are often significant in the lives of the families undergoing therapy, can sabotage the therapeutic process and hinder access to the family.

CREATION OF WORKABLE REALITIES

Taken from structural family therapy (Minuchin, 1974; Minuchin & Fishman, 1981), the construction of workable realities has been defined as the process in which the family's view of the problem is transformed from a paradigm of individual causality (he or she is to blame) to a paradigm of interaction (we can work together to remedy this problem). Through the process of joining, using language, enacting, and reframing, the clinician introduces family members to a view of the problem that differs enough from their own to provide opportunities for new interpersonal transactions (Minuchin & Fishman, 1981). This is not a sequential process, however; clinicians weave the parts of the process together to create this new workable reality.

Discovering the Facts

In the beginning stage of therapy, the therapist is not concerned with discovering the "truth," because truth is relative in social systems. Families with symptomatic members share a world view or truth that limits the possibility for change. The therapist must broaden the family's reality into a broader world view, a problem-solving paradigm, without compromising either the family's or the therapist's values. This problem-solving paradigm explains the framework of a workable reality.

One couple brought their family to therapy because of marital problems. The couple had been together for 21 years and had been at war with each other for all of those 21 years. Entering therapy, they asked the therapist to solve their marital problems. As the therapist helped them with their marital problems, the long, ceaseless stream of low-keyed marital squabbling continued. Fundamental change could not occur, because the family's belief that they have marital problems is limiting their ability to talk together. Almost by accident, the mother mentioned that the oldest son, 16, had a drug problem. As the therapist delved into this, it became clear that the father was minimizing his son's drug problem because he did not want to jeopardize his relationship with the boy. The therapist then used the frame "Your son has a drug problem; how will you parents solve it?" to elicit cooperative behavior from the parents. By constructing this workable reality, the therapist helped the parents to do in one frame (talk and work together) what they could not do in another. The couple had strengths as parents that they did not use as spouses. These parental strengths allowed them to plan and work together (organize) so that they could solve the problem (their son's drug abuse).

In the construction of each new workable reality that effectively achieves the goal of redefining the problem, the framework emphasizes strengths rather than deficits, shifts the family's reality to a broader world view that allows new behavioral alternatives, and clearly indicates what people should do (organize) to make things different. Breunlin and Cimmarusti (1983) described the paradigm as follows: "You, the family, using such-and-such strengths can function (organize) in such-and-such a way, and in doing so the problem you have presented, framed in such-and-such a way, will be solved" (p. 286).

In order to construct a workable frame from which the family can build an improved reality, the therapist must make an interactional assessment and diagnosis. This is a fluid, ongoing process that moves from initial hypothesis about life events, culture, composition, class, and context to the interpersonal arena of the family-therapist system. The interactional diagnosis is based on the present. In making this diagnosis, the therapist takes into account different classes of information, including verbal and nonverbal cues, and the fact that what is *not* happening may be more important than what is happening. The therapist is constantly going through a circular process: forming a hypothesis; testing it through observation and intervention; confirming, modifying, or refuting the hypothesis; setting and implementing goals; and, finally, modifying goals based on feedback from the family (Colapinto & Lappin, 1982).

Creating Change

The leap from discovering the "facts" to creating change in a family can be quite a jump. It is helpful if the therapist can do one thing while thinking another. When meeting the family for the first time, the therapist must respect the family members' desire to tell their story. While listening to the parent, the therapist should also observe the process; for example, the child may play noisily and distract the parent, who may respond with an angry command and then give the child a hug as he cries. Unless the therapist becomes comfortable with this kind of double vision, chances are that he or she will miss invaluable process information.

As the leader of the therapeutic system, the therapist must exercise some judgment about punctuating content and process; otherwise, opportunities to construct workable realities may be lost. Although it is preferable for the therapist to follow content and process simultaneously by means of double vision, the therapist must often make a choice between the two. It is important to keep in mind the concept of joining and look for feedback from family members regarding their perceptions of the therapist's understanding of their situation. Therapists tend to believe that the family is reactant when family members keep saying, "You don't understand." Sometimes it is reactance, but often, the therapist has not listened.

Most choices in therapy involve timing. It would be a mistake to describe a misbehaving adolescent as "confused" in the first few minutes of therapy, before family members have had a chance to tell their story and before the therapist has established credibility. Even if the frame fits the family, using it too soon will decrease its effectiveness, because it will be easier for the family to dismiss it. The therapist needs patience. Some families can move quickly, while others progress much more slowly; this is true for therapists as well. Therapists can experiment with the appropriate pace, both for themselves and for the families that they are treating, if they keep an eye on the dynamic nature of the beginning stage, the goal and tasks, and the need for joining.

While therapists should enter the first session with preconceived hypotheses about an interactional diagnosis of the family, such hypotheses should be abandoned if feedback from the family affords a more workable hypothesis. Otherwise, the therapist is operating from an agenda that does not apply to the family. Consequently, the therapist could be imposing a preconceived frame on the family rather than developing one from the family situation. The therapist observes the family member–family member and the family-therapist interactions, searching for patterns (sequences) and relationships (structures). Frames that evolve from these interactions are connected to the family.

Once a good working frame has been developed, the family must agree to it. Highly skilled therapists can often weave together the various tasks of the beginning stage and are joined so well with the family that they develop the frame and elicit agreement simultaneously. There are other ways in which therapists can ensure a family's agreement with the workable reality, however. The therapist may simply obtain overt agreement to the more workable reality, for example. This approach may lack elegance, but it compensates for this in directness. Perhaps with the majority of families, the therapist seeks this overt confirmation.

Families may indicate their agreement to the new frame through their willingness to accept the therapist's leadership. Beginning therapists, especially, may feel uncomfortable with this leadership role, but they should recognize that it is a valid way to confirm a reality. Families may also accept the workable reality as a revelation, as a new piece of information. On these occasions, the new reality generates considerable energy in the family. No matter how a family signals its acceptance of the workable reality, the therapist must be alert to the clues that the family is in agreement. An accepted workable reality initiates the process of change and signals the completion of the beginning stage. When things go well, the beginning stage may be completed in the first session. Often, however, the first interview must be devoted to making a connection with the family. Therapists must remember their tasks and goal when the beginning stage is protracted in order to have a direction and purpose.

OUT-OF-SESSION ISSUES

Family therapists treat family systems, but these systems function within a larger context that includes other persons who may be providing services to the family. In many cases involving multiproblem families that are being serviced by many agencies, the therapist must create alternative realities with a number of people just to gain unencumbered access to the family. When a family is experiencing problems on a number of fronts, such as school, court, or welfare system, the therapist must organize each so as to be free to work with the family without fear that the school counselor will expel the child, the court will place the child in a foster home, or the welfare department will cut off the family's allotment. Therapists must remember that these other service providers can play an important part in the family. They may, for example, interact with the family in a way that emphasizes deficits, encourages dependence, or in some other way fosters a dysfunctional family organization. A well-intentioned child welfare worker, for instance, may unwittingly place a child with an overly intrusive relative and then be organized to treat the mother as if she were incompetent.

Working with Other Service Providers

The goal of working with other service providers is not to change them, but to ensure the therapist's free access to the family. This is accomplished by creating workable realities with these other providers (i.e., by joining, using language, and reframing). In many cases, their perception of the family's problem is also punctuated in a way that prevents them from being able to help the family. For example, the school counselor may see Johnny as emotionally disturbed and his parents as dull and disinterested; therefore, the counselor may give up trying to do anything for Johnny except to find a specialist who is trained to work with disturbed children. Likewise, the child welfare worker may see the family as "bad" and may recommend long-term placement of the child in a foster home because the family is "beyond hope" and "can't change."

By offering these service providers an alternative reality, the therapist not only gives them new behavioral opportunities, but also keeps them from sabotaging the therapy (Carl & Jurkovic, 1983). Creating a workable reality with the school counselor that Johnny is lazy, not disturbed, offers the counselor a problem that he or she can solve; more important, it buys the therapist time to work. Also, convincing the child welfare worker that the family is dysfunctional, not bad, may decrease pressure on the family, result in fewer family-worker transactions that reinforce the message of "badness" to the family, and again buy time for therapy.

In approaching other service providers, it is necessary to determine their position vis-à-vis the family in three areas: (1) their interest in the family, (2) their potential control over the family, and (3) their agenda for the family's involvement in therapy. From this information the therapist can determine the importance of working with this person and the amount of work to be done.

Family therapists should realize that other service providers often have a great deal of interest in their clients and may even have an investment in a certain therapy outcome. At the very least, an interested service provider needs information from the therapist. A service provider who makes recommendations to a legal authority that might affect the family's boundaries or sense of security may assert considerable countrol over the family. A child welfare worker, for example, who represents the state and can make recommendations about the placement of the child, has this control. Control may also be based on perceived influence. Thus, a teacher, who has little direct control over a family, has considerable influence because of the importance of school.

The other service provider's agenda includes not only the desired outcome of therapy, but also the relationship of the provider with the therapist. Some providers have a personal interest in the therapy, which can create competition between the therapist and the other service provider. Occasionally, because of preconceived notions about therapists and therapy or because of a desire to appear competent, service providers tell therapists what they believe the therapists want to hear. When this occurs, the therapist may not learn of the service provider's frustration and readiness to give up on the family; consequently, the therapist may misjudge the service provider's impact on the family.

For example, therapists who receive cases from state child welfare services meet caseworkers who have varying degrees of interest in the families, who have considerable legal authority and influence on the families, and who have an agenda for what "should" happen to the families. It is a mistake to ignore these caseworkers. Involvement with them is an important part of providing service to the family. Creating a working relationship with these caseworkers may require considerable joining and framing skills.

Usually, other service providers are willing to help the therapist with the family if the therapist takes the time to explain what needs to be done and why. Unfortunately, some family therapists treat other service providers as if they were incompetent and ignore them. These therapists lose an excellent opportunity to gather information and obtain assistance from the other providers.

Drawing Hypotheses

In order to begin the first session in a purposeful way, the therapist must draw hypotheses beforehand. The process begins with intake information and is refined again and again as the therapist meets with other service providers and the family. When refined and used carefully, hypotheses provide a way to screen data, maintain the direction of therapy, and tap family strengths. They keep the clinician in the process of double vision. As the family interacts the therapist can listen while seeking confirmation or refutation of hypotheses through answers to the following questions:

- What are the boundaries?
- Who talks to whom about what? When, how often, and with what results?
- What is the family hierarchy?
- Are there coalitions?
- To the degree one member is involved, who might be more distant?
- Is it a flexible system?
- Is the current problem a temporary disturbance in the family life cycle, or is it a chronic way of living?
- What is the general feel of the family?
- What possible repetitive patterns could maintain the dysfunction?

Clinicians cannot draw appropriate hypotheses unless they understand the effect of life cycle events on both the individual and the family as a system. For example, it is not enough to know that adolescence is a tumultuous period. The therapist must be aware that the combination of an adolescent and two parents who are going through midlife crises approaches a critical mass. Without this knowledge, therapists are destined to test only prefabricated hypotheses (e.g., every father is peripheral, all mothers are enmeshed). Such prefabricated hypotheses impede the process of the beginning stage by blinding the therapist's double vision. Under these circumstances, therapy becomes a struggle to prove the rightness of a hypothesis, and the therapist becomes a slave to that hypothesis.

While hypotheses are useful, the interaction of family members with each other and the therapist is the most important source of data. While ongoing out-of-session work is necessary, it is only valuable insofar as the therapist can utilize it in the sessions.

IN-SESSION ISSUES

The tasks of the beginning stage of therapy (i.e., engage, assess the problem, set goals, and initiate the process of change) are not always completed by the end of the first session. If a family is suspicious of therapy, the therapist may find it difficult to do more in the first session than help the family relax. A secretive family may keep the therapist at arm's length during the first session. With families from certain cultural groups, the therapist must move slowly, lest they be offended. Sometimes, it is just not possible to test hypotheses or to obtain the information necessary to build a workable reality. Clearly, it takes time for the family-therapist system to evolve. Expecting to create a workable reality in the first 15 minutes of the first session, and to then restructure the family in the next half hour, leaving 15 minutes to terminate, is an admirable but unrealistic goal for therapy. If the therapist can join the family at the first session, there will be ample opportunities to "conduct therapy."

Minuchin and Fishman (1981) have asserted that "joining a family is more an attitude than a technique, and it is the umbrella under which all therapeutic transactions occur" (p. 31). All too frequently, beginning clinicians see joining only as the first stage in the therapy process. As they test the flexibility of a family system, however, they may discover that early social encounters are not enough to sustain a relationship with family members and that good joining is not an absolute quality attached to certain specific behaviors of the therapist or to a specific stage of treatment. Joining is a means to an end; the therapist must join the family system if he or she is going to help it to change.

Effective joining offers challenge and hope. Challenges to the family must be accompanied by a message of hope. The therapist conveys hope to the family partly through the actual challenges and partly through respectfulness for the family, curiosity about the family, playfulness with the family, and clinical self-confidence. It is good joining (Colapinto & Lappin, 1982) to say to a mother who is unsuccessfully trying to get her 4-year-old daughter to sit quietly, "It is not working" (Minuchin & Colapinto, 1980). It immediately connects with the mother, who knows better than anyone that she is failing to manage the child. At the same time, it challenges the mother to be effective and assumes that she will be. Thus, the therapist implicitly notes her competence, giving hope.

Joining is not a prescription (Colapinto & Lappin, 1982), but is doing what it takes for the therapist to gain a position of influence within the family. At the end of the first session, the family should feel that the decision to seek treatment was a good one. The therapist must offer enough confirmation of the family's reality to make the family feel that "this person understands." Joining is a highly idiosyncratic activity that involves the style of the therapist, the reality of the family, and the larger social context that organizes both. The therapist must not only read the system's feedback, but also must be tuned into his or her personal feedback.

It is invaluable for the therapist to be inducted into the family's reality, albeit briefly. Momentary inductions give the therapist an inner sense of being, for example, the scapegoated child or the frustrated parent. This process taps areas of the therapist's self that facilitate the process of joining.

A therapist, suddenly feeling angry over the father's silence in the session, turned and asked the mother if it upset her that her husband was so quiet. Although the mother disagreed with the statement, the therapist noticed that the daughter frowned when the question was asked. Turning to the mother again, the therapist asked if perhaps the daughter was upset over her father's silence. Suddenly, the mother's eyes filled with tears as she related her sadness over the highly conflicted relationship between father and daughter.

Thus, the therapist can use an inducted response to the family in order to gain access to the family's reality, produce connections, and begin building a more workable reality. From this inducted position, the therapist can understand the family's anguish over the problem, search for the family's strengths, and develop effective interventions and frames. The therapist should not become the family's emotional magnet, however, because that would restrict the therapist's ability to produce change. Nevertheless, knowing a family beyond its cybernetic components is productive.

Ultimately, the therapist's attitude may determine the success of the beginning stage of therapy. A therapist who has an attitude of hope, respect, and curiosity is more likely to negotiate the beginning stage complexities successfully than is a therapist who feels hopeless, overwhelmed, and overburdened. The former therapist will exude patience and tolerance when the family fails to follow the steps of therapy. The latter therapist will be impatient and unwilling to accept the unique responses of the family.

REFERENCES

Breunlin, D.C., & Cimmarusti, R.A. (1983). Seven opportunities for brief therapy: A recipe for rapid change. In L. Wolberg & M. Aronson (Eds.), *Group and family therapy 1983* (pp. 282–295). New York: Brunner/Mazel.

Carl D., & Jurkovic, G.J. (1983). Agency triangles: Problems in agency–family relationships. *Family Process, 22*:441–451.

Colapinto, T., & Lappin, J. (1982). *Joining revisited.* Unpublished manuscript.

Goldstein, S.E. (1945). *Marriage and family counseling.* New York: McGraw Hill.

Haley, J. (1976). *Problem-solving therapy.* San Francisco: Jossey Bass.

Minuchin, S. (1974). *Families and family therapy.* Cambridge, Mass.: Harvard University Press.

Minuchin, S., & Colapinto, J. (1980). *Taming monsters* (Videotape). Philadelphia: Philadelphia Child Guidance Clinic.

Minuchin, S., & Fishman, H.C. (1981). *Family therapy techniques.* Cambridge, Mass.: Harvard University Press.

Satir, V. (1964). *Conjoint family therapy: A guide to theory and techniques.* Palo Alto, Calif.: Science and Behavior Books.

Selvini-Palazzoli, M., Boscolo, L., Cecchin, G., & Prata, G. (1978). *Paradox and counterparadox.* New York: Jason Aronson.

Watzlawick, P., Weakland, J., & Fisch, R. (1974). *Change: Principles of problem formulation and problem resolution.* New York: W.W. Norton.

Weakland, T., Fisch, R., Watzlawick, P., & Bodin, A. (1974). Brief therapy: Focused problem resolution. *Family Process, 13*, 141–168.

3. The Middle Phase: The Evolving Process of Change

Dennis McGuire

I'm not at the beginning and I'm not at the end, so it must be the middle phase.

J. Fouts (Psych. Intern, 1983/84)

In the middle phase of therapy, initial changes are consolidated and families prepared to terminate treatment. In spite of its importance, the middle phase is virtually ignored in the literature. As Umbarger (1983) stated, "Family therapy often seems an exercise in brilliant openings and happy outcomes with little in between worth mentioning" (p. 143). For example, strategic therapists generally advocate an end to therapy once the presenting problem has been eliminated, and structural therapists, with a few notable exceptions (e.g., Combrinck-Graham, Gursky, & Brendler, 1982; Umbarger, 1983), rarely discuss the middle phase in their writings.

The reasons for this omission are not entirely clear. Theoreticians may consider the middle phase so complicated or ambiguous that it eludes formulation and encapsulation within a defined treatment approach. It may be ignored because the familiarity between family and therapist in the middle phase exposes too many of the therapist's vulnerabilities. Others may fear that the middle phase represents some vestige of traditional psychiatry in which a person's failure to change quickly is considered evidence of a deep-seated problem and an indication that the person may never change at all.

In order to determine whether the middle phase is a legitimate concept in family therapy, I conducted an informal survey, asking more than 40 clinicians to comment on the middle phase. Almost all these clinicians acknowledged a middle phase in their practices, and most identified this phase as the most difficult period of therapy. Moreover, there was a general lack of confidence in their ability to manage the process of treatment effectively beyond the opening moves and a consensus that their interventions in the middle phase lacked form or focus. It may be concluded from this survey that the middle phase is a reality that demands closer scrutiny and formal description. Practitioners need concrete guidelines and treatment strategies for the middle phase. As these clinicians report, the lack of these guidelines and strategies negatively affects treatment outcomes.

Three key variables of the systemic approach can be extended and applied to the evolving process of change in the middle phase: belief system, structure, and development. A belief system is defined as one's language and view of the world (Minuchin, 1974). In the context of treatment this centers on how problems and solutions are formulated to promote change. Structure refers to the family network and is based on a generationally organized hierarchy (Haley, 1977; Minuchin, 1974). Finally, development can be defined as the normal process of growth and change through the life cycle for individuals, relationships, and the family as a whole (Haley, 1973).

DEFINITION AND PARAMETERS

The middle phase of family therapy may be analyzed both as a distinct entity and as a part of the entire therapeutic process. Unlike the beginning and ending phases, which involve a number of popular and tested intervention strategies that clinicians may use with relative confidence, the middle phase is distinguished by the need for clinicians to respond creatively to the infinite number of variations that are unique to each family's reality and circumstances. The middle phase is guided by what has occurred in the beginning phase and what is expected to occur in the ending phase, however. Thus, there is already a tentative map and structure from which to explore and build subsequent interventions with an end or final goal in mind.

It may be assumed that the middle phase begins when the opening series of interventions, focusing on the presenting problem or a related structural difficulty, is completed and ends when the therapist or family initiates a process of disengagement from the therapeutic process. Although this definition is valid in optimal situations, it generates a number of dilemmas. For example, can there be a middle phase if there is no substantive change in the beginning phase? Moreover, can the middle phase be a legitimate phase if its end result is not adaptive functioning, but family dependency on the therapist?

FORMULA FOR CHANGE IN THE MIDDLE PHASE

While it is not possible to offer solutions for all circumstances and problems, we will propose a formula for assessing the conditions that are necessary and sufficient to produce substantive change in and throughout the middle phase. Such conditions can be determined by examining the family's belief system, structure, and development, as defined earlier, and by relating each to resistance to change. The goal of treatment is to produce a family structure that is stable, yet flexible enough to adjust to the changing environment and the exigencies of the developmental process.

Given this formula, the middle phase may involve a number of possible strategies, depending on the severity of the problem and the skill of the therapist. For some families, there is no need to go beyond an opening series of sessions in order to achieve substantive change; for others, the beginning focus (e.g., on a child) may be an entree into a much more serious exploration (e.g., in the marital subsystem) that calls for extensive middle-phase interventions. For still other families, interventions that are appropriate at the start of the middle phase may not be appropriate as treatment draws to a close. For example, a clinician may effectively block a child from a marital problem, but have difficulty personally disengaging from a mediating position as treatment progresses toward termination. In this case, the clinician has merely traded places with the child who had previously monitored this marital relationship, and treatment continues indefinitely. The success of treatment in the middle phase depends on the skill of the clinician in assessing the scope and duration of interventions necessary to promote substantive change.

The formula helps clinicians avoid any one of three stances that prohibit change in the middle phase of therapy: uncompromising, too compromising, and ad infinitum. In the uncompromising stance, the clinician dictates the conditions or parameters of treatment by making demands, such as insisting that an absent member be present or that hidden marital problems be discussed. In doing so, the clinician fails to adapt to the family's response to the ongoing therapy. The therapist may assume this stance, which often causes the family to discontinue treatment, when he or she has had some success in the beginning phase but has misjudged the family's reaction to more sensitive issues, such as marital problems. The uncompromising stance also occurs when the therapist continues to push directly on the family's resistance rather than shifting to an indirect approach that would be more effective. Finally, the stance in some cases represents the last move of a frustrated and exasperated clinician.

In the too compromising stance, the clinician nullifies therapeutic leverage by being too flexible or accommodating. This is a particular danger for inexperienced clinicians who too readily accept the family's description of a problem as unchangeable (Dell, 1980). Typically, these clinicians are inconsistent, attempting various interventions without using any one for a long enough period to determine whether it is effective. The results of this stance are variable. Sometimes families discontinue treatment. In other cases, families continue treatment for years, becoming "known to agencies" and being passed from student to student as "good learning cases."

The clinician in the ad infinitum stance does not try hard enough to promote change and, thus, may be lulled into a pattern of weekly sessions that are without form, substance, or vitality. This stance is a particular problem for clinicians who wish to feel needed and are reluctant to challenge the status of the therapeutic alliance lest the family terminate therapy. These clinicians may focus on a key issue but detour when change is imminent, or they may choose to focus an issue that is of minor significance—either approach prevents substantive change.

Belief System

Beliefs represent the framework or general scaffolding on which the two other variables, structure and development, rest. Problems may arise in this area during the middle phase of family therapy, however. Both the therapist's and the family's beliefs must be considered. First, familiarity between family and therapist during the middle phase is more apt to expose the therapist's personal vulnerabilities. This not only may divert the focus from family issues, but also may inhibit or instill uncertainty into the therapist. Second, the middle phase presents an infinite number of possible directions that the therapist may pursue, but there is little guidance in the literature. Third, the therapist may become less objective and more susceptible to the family's beliefs over the course of treatment. Finally, many clients consider symptoms fixed internal phenomena; for these individuals, each incidence of the problem behavior reaffirms their view that the problem is an unchangeable entity (Dell, 1980). Thus, once past the excitement and novelty of the opening moves, the therapist may move from optimism to frustration and despair over a family-held belief that does not allow for change.

The biblical account of the exodus is an interesting metaphor for the middle phase of family therapy. The opening moves of the exodus were quite spectacular: fire, pestilence, and even a parting of the Red Sea. In the desert, however, when the Israelites were still a long way from the Promised Land, the middle phase began to plague Moses. After bearing many weeks of complaints, loss of faith, idol worship, and the like, Moses "cried to the Lord" in desperation, "what shall I do with these people; another day and they will stone me" (Exodus 17:4). Yahweh directed Moses to "go before the people and take with you three of the elders of Israel and thy staff" (the symbol of authority; Exodus 17:5). In effect, Yahweh recommended to Moses what therapists should do in the middle phase:

1. Look and act like a leader.
2. Maintain the frame and focus in the face of pressure to succumb to a less acceptable problem definition/world view (be it an idol or an internal deficit).
3. Enlist the help of a respectable consultant (elder) to give support, when necessary, or to lend a new perspective to the problem.

Structural Issues

In assessing the organizational makeup of the family network, the therapist must remember that a single symptom may reflect difficulties in and across various network levels (Haley, 1977). For example, a child's school failure may reflect disagreement between the parents about homework completion, which may mirror a marital conflict. This marital problem may involve an interfering relative, such as a grandparent who sides with one parent in the homework dispute. The child's failure may also be an indication of a family-school disagreement over the amount or need for homework. Changes in any one of these structures during treatment may reveal or affect the difficulties in the other levels.

In constructing appropriate treatment strategies, the clinician must determine when and how to focus on the different levels to effect change. Throughout therapy, the clinician should focus on the structural level at which therapy will produce the greatest amount of change with the least amount of resistance. In the beginning phase, clinicians often concentrate on the presenting problem and those structures most involved in the problem. For some families, this not only may resolve the presenting problem, but also may produce substantive change across all levels of the structure, thus making further treatment unnecessary. For other families, however, an initial change in structure necessitates a focus in the middle phase on an inadequate or emerging structure.

Failure to assess all structural levels may have serious repercussions on the treatment process. Therapy with partial structures is like marriage counseling with one partner missing—the therapist may not have sufficient leverage or data to effect change. Treatment may end abruptly, or it may go on indefinitely because the therapist has overlooked factors that may offset any positive gains made in therapy.

In most cases, even if other structural problems are minimized or blocked, the marriage poses the most difficult questions of timing and strategy. Focusing too quickly on the marriage may precipitate an untimely termination of therapy. On the other hand, failing to take advantage of an opening to the marriage may ensure the continuation or reemergence of the presenting problem, particularly if the problem is a child's symptom that regulates intimacy or conflict between the parents. In order to ensure that the timing of therapy directed to the marriage is appropriate, the clinician should initially focus on a narrow band of behavior surrounding the presenting problem (e.g., the child's homework activity), later expanding the focus to include the issues of cooperation and consistency between parents around the child's behavior. The clinician can move toward a more direct interpretation of the marital conflict as the couple experiences some success in working together vis-à-vis the child.

The inclusion of individuals who are not an immediate part of the problem context can enhance the therapeutic process in the middle phase. For example, a college-aged child may have the right amount of objectivity and understanding to help resolve a problem with a younger sibling at home. Similarly, the inclusion of the couple's parents in marital therapy often adds depth and meaning to a couple's understanding of issues or styles related to the partner's family of origin. Although such flexibility and creativity are possible in the middle phase, they might have been viewed by some as inappropriate eclecticism in the beginning phase.

Developmental Issues

If therapy is successful, it sets the process of growth and development into motion once again. Just as treatment in the middle phase focuses on different structural levels, it must focus on a range of developmental issues. It is important to assess carefully the developmental needs of individual family members. For example, a child who has been disengaged from a problem-maintaining position in the home-school network may have fallen so far behind in academics that he or she needs special tutoring. Similarly, the child may have been disengaged from peers and thus may benefit from a group experience or from some individual counseling to build social skills. Even though therapy may block symptomatic young adults from their involvement in the marriage, they are not always ready for independent living. Thus, individual therapy, group therapy, or even job counseling sessions may be needed to help them leave home successfully. Couples, too, may find that they need help in learning to reestablish intimacy once their children have moved out of their marriage.

The amount of resistance and the difficulty of therapeutic interventions in the marriage are determined by the severity or chronicity of the problem. For example, a child's symptom may have regulated an oscillating pattern of proximity and distance in a marriage. Because such a pattern is often more extreme and of longer duration for less adaptive families, a pattern of disengagement in such a family may not be apparent until well into the middle phase of therapy. At this point, the therapist may be baffled by parental conflict accompanied by a robust reonset of the symptom. Therapists, however, may understand and manage this pattern if they (1) are prepared for it, (2) predict its occurrence, and (3) intervene to block the extremes of this oscillation and allow a new more adaptive middle range of behavior to emerge.

The disengagement of both a symptomatic child and interfering grandparents from the marital subsystem created a major crisis in a couple's relationship. The wife reported anxiety attacks, and the therapist traced them to feelings of overcloseness and disengagement within the couple's relationship. To challenge this pattern, the therapist instructed the husband to coach his wife through these periods with patient, but not overly solicitous, attention. This allowed a new, more comfortable and functional midrange of closeness in the couple. In time, as the couple began to trust this new intimacy, the wife's anxiety attacks began to dissipate. In follow-up meetings, the therapist helped the couple use this more adaptive connectedness to weather a number of crises, including a brief reappearance of the child's symptom and the repeated recurrence of this pattern of estrangement.

CONCLUSION

In family therapy, the goal of treatment is to forge an optimal fit or balance between the internal and external needs and demands of a family network. In order to facilitate this process, therapists must be able to organize and predict the process of therapy well beyond the initial phase of treatment. A solid theoretical understanding of the family's belief system, structure, and development, coupled with a renewed confidence in the therapist's ability to promote change, permits effective handling of the middle phase.

REFERENCES

Combrinck-Graham, L., Gursky, E., & Brendler, J. (1982). Hospitalization of single parent families of disturbed adolescents. *Family Process,* 141–152.

Dell, P. (1980). The Hopi family therapist and the Aristotelian parents. *Journal of Marital and Family Therapy* (6) 123–130.

Haley, J. (1973). *Uncommon therapy*. New York: Ballantine Books.

Haley, J. (1977). *Problem-solving therapy*. San Francisco: Jossey Bass.

Minuchin, S. (1974). *Families and family therapy*. Cambridge, Mass.: Harvard University Press.

Umbarger, C. (1983). *Structural family therapy*. New York: Grune & Stratton.

4. Ending Family Therapy: Some New Directions

Anthony W. Heath

The family entered the therapy room for the last time. Everyone, including the therapist, knew it would be so. They had discussed this final meeting in the previous two sessions and were now prepared to part with each other. They all agreed that the therapy had been a success and that now was the time to terminate.

The group reviewed the major events in the therapy. The therapist congratulated first the parents, then the children, on their efforts. The parents, in turn, thanked the therapist for her help. Everyone joked about the extra hour they would have in their schedules next week. Closing the door as the family left the office, the therapist jotted a few notes in the family's file and placed it in the termination basket. Feeling warm but melancholy, she turned off the lights and left for home.

Even in private practice, few cases end so civilly. Usually, they end with a last minute cancellation or a no-show and several telephone calls. Agency clients tend to drop out long before any changes in family structure or function become apparent, leaving therapists to wonder what happened as they fill out the termination summary weeks later. When serious problems remain in the family, a therapist's wonder can turn to dread. Furthermore, therapists may feel that every unplanned termination is a failure of their therapeutic abilities.

The practice of medicine offers a model of the termination process that can relieve family therapists' guilt over unplanned terminations and guide their efforts in some difficult situations. Unfortunately, the model is not easily used in certain settings or by therapists of some theoretical orientations. Nevertheless, it is clear that, in certain situations, the new model can encourage terminations that are more satisfactory for all concerned. Those who can put aside the traditional biases of family therapists will find that this is one specific area in which medical practice can advance family therapy.

The author sincerely thanks Douglas Breunlin, Thomas Ayers, and David Norton for their help in developing the ideas expressed in this article.

33

TERMINATION IN MEDICAL PRACTICE

People go to physicians when their problems become too painful, in a physical or emotional sense, to be endured any longer. As patients, they receive treatment and leave the office, scheduling future visits as recommended by the physician. Not all appointments are kept by patients, however, regardless of the seriousness of the medical problem. Some patients simply do not comply with the physician's orders. Such noncompliance must be attributable to (1) a reduction of pain to a tolerable level as a result of the treatment received during the previous visit, (2) an increase in the threshold of tolerable pain owing to fear of additional diagnosis or treatment, or (3) dissatisfaction with services provided. Physicians are concerned by patients' noncompliance with their advice, partly because of legal liabilities, and they typically have their assistants try to reschedule cancelled and missed appointments.

People go to therapists when the subjective pain of their emotional and interpersonal problems exceeds a tolerable level. Like physicians' patients, but probably to a lesser extent, clients schedule future appointments as recommended by their therapist. At this juncture, as in medical practice, clients decide whether to comply with the therapist's advice. Should clients fail to comply with a directive to return for other appointments, the therapist must assume that (1) the clients' subjective pain has been reduced to a tolerable level, (2) they fear additional treatment, or (3) they are dissatisfied with the services provided. Like physicians, therapists often attempt to contact their reluctant clients to reschedule missed appointments.

Thus, family therapy is very similar to outpatient medical practice in that people request, receive, and refuse services in similar ways and for similar reasons, carrying similar expectations and hestitations. Even physicians and therapists respond to their "customers" in basically similar ways, specifically in the beginnings and endings of treatment. These similarities make it possible for family therapists to use the ideas and approaches of physicians in dealing with the difficulties of termination.

Five aspects of the medical practice model of termination are particularly applicable to family therapy:

1. Because clients see therapy as similar to medical treatment, therapists should respond to their clients as would a caring, reliable physician, respecting clients' right to monitor their own "health" and providing firm guidance when necessary.
2. The three distinct explanations for client noncompliance suggest several interventions to guide the therapists' response to unexpected terminations.
3. Variable intervals can be used in therapy, as suggested by Selvini-Palazzoli (1980). Like physicians, brief therapists schedule sessions separated by

intervals of increasing length (Fisch, Weakland, & Segal, 1982) as subjective pain lessens and problems diminish. In the final sense of the word, termination never occurs in brief therapy, as it never occurs in medical practice.

4. Therapists can alleviate client despair by encouraging clients to return should the problem recur.

5. Therapists should realize the importance of customer satisfaction in maintaining a personal or agency clientele. They should identify and respect client expectations or "positions" for each visit (Fisch et al., 1982), and they should be willing to explain any treatment approach that differs from that anticipated by the client. For example, many clients expect a diagnosis and a prescription from their therapist in the first session, as they expect the same from their physician. Wise therapists either provide some semblance of the client expectation or justify their actions.

The adoption of the medical practice model of termination requires a reconsideration of the meanings of two basic terms, *therapy* and *termination*. Therapy is commonly thought of as a series of sessions; the expression "they are in therapy" implies that clients attend therapy sessions regularly. This new model challenges that assumption, because according to the model, sessions are usually held as requested by the clients. Just as an individual becomes a "patient" of a physician after one office visit, he or she becomes a "client" of a therapist after one session. Thus, the term *therapy* loses much of its traditional meaning. Similarly, the word *termination* cannot be used in the usual way, because most clients now enter and exit therapy according to their immediate needs. Perhaps the plural form *terminations* should replace the singular form to describe the overall enter-exit-reenter sequence; the word *termination* could be used, if necessary, to refer to the session preceding an indefinite pause.

INDICATIONS AND CONTRAINDICATIONS

In general, the medical practice model of termination is most appealing to problem-focused therapists, because it fits into their consumerist, constructivist (Watzlawick, 1984) assumptions about clients, problems, and therapy. The problem-focused models of family therapy, such as the brief therapy articulated by representatives of the Mental Research Institute Brief Therapy Center (Fisch et al., 1982; Watzlawick, Weakland, & Fisch, 1974), promote respectful treatment of the "customers" of therapy. Problem-focused therapists believe that clients are doing their absolute best to solve practical problems; these therapists do not assume pathology and tend to intervene as little as possible. As Haley (1967) observed of Milton Erickson, this willingness to see therapy as less than a process leading to a total cure allows clients to leave therapy according to their own judgment and without regard for any diagnoses applied by any professionals.

Other theories of family therapy do not accommodate the medical practice model as easily. Many growth-oriented family therapists, for example, perceive psychological deficits in families and seek to correct them, which takes more time than does what they might call "simple relief of symptoms." Clients who leave therapy before achieving the therapist's goals are considered treatment failures. Under the medical practice model, however, these clients are not necessarily treatment failures; instead, they are satisfied customers who have received what they wanted—a reduction in emotional pain. Growth-oriented therapists could use the model to describe a "prematurely lost" case as a failure to convince the client of the diagnosis or of the value of the prescribed treatment.

The treatment setting also affects the applicability of the medical practice model of termination. Private practices with scheduling flexibility seem most clearly able to accommodate the unpredictable nature of client exits from and reentries to therapy. Agencies rarely have such flexibility of therapist time. On the other hand, if all the noncustomers and therapy "groupies" who occupy therapists' time were managed according to the model, more time would be available for two-session consultations and returns by satisfied clients with new problems. The circularity of this circumstance merely illustrates the political nature of therapists' schedules and should not proscribe the use of the model.

The medical practice model of termination applies equally well to clients with mild problems and to those with serious problems, such as substance abuse and violence. Therapists who are using this model will strongly advise clients with dangerous difficulties to get help from a professional, offering their services when appropriate. Once the recommendations have been made, however, the clients are free to follow them or to ignore them. The freedom allowed to clients by the medical practice model may concern some therapists, especially when clients who have serious problems decide to discontinue therapy. While most experienced physicians and therapists respect the basic right of individuals and families to refuse treatment, many referral sources expect continuous therapy for those with serious problems. Thus therapists who use the medical practice model must devise ways to deal with the expectations of their referral sources.

APPLICATION OF THE MEDICAL PRACTICE MODEL

In order to be maximally useful, the medical practice model of termination must help the therapist to terminate therapy when it is in the long-range best interest of clients. More specifically, the model must be consistent with the therapist's plan for treatment and establish the therapist (or facility) as a resource to which clients can return, if necessary.

Preliminary Groundwork

The termination process begins in the first session of therapy when the therapist unveils the treatment plan. Clients appreciate hearing a preliminary diagnosis or hypothesis about their situation and want to know how the treatment will proceed. This simple process seems to alleviate fears of withheld diagnoses and unmentionable treatment methods, one of the three major reasons for unexpected terminations.

As part of the treatment plan disclosure, the therapist should estimate the number of sessions that will be required to achieve the goals of therapy. Tact is essential in recommending additional sessions. Some clients appreciate the professional's advice, but others, including many of those with serious problems, consider it interference and resist it. For the difficult question of how to entice hesitant clients to return to therapy, there are no simple answers. Simply telling such clients how therapy would help them resolve their "problems" and asking them to call if they would like to return is sometimes sufficient.

Therapists should appear reasonably certain of their hypotheses in order to establish professional credibility. Hypotheses should not substantially reduce the clients' problem-related pain, however, unless the session is to be a one-time consultation. Positive connotations of difficult circumstances, for example, should be avoided at first, because they reduce both client pain and motivation to continue therapy. As the medical practice model of termination suggests, pain reduction promotes unexpected terminations.

Therapists can assign tasks in the first session, just as physicians issue prescriptions. Even if the task is a generic one, such as collecting baseline data on the problem, people seem pleased to receive a concrete prescription in their first session. All these actions help to prevent unexpected termination because of clients' dissatisfaction with the outcome of their sessions.

Planned Terminations

In an ideal world, the clinician is able to anticipate each termination in family therapy. Anticipation allows planning, and planning allows therapy to be used to the fullest advantage of clients (Haley, 1976). Under the medical practice model of termination, however, not all terminations can be planned, because clients enter, exit, and reenter therapy largely as they please. Nevertheless, terminations can be regulated through a number of actions, especially with clients who generally comply with "doctor's orders:"

1. At the earliest signs of progress in therapy, such as therapist boredom, symptom swapping, and extended social interchanges with clients in ses-

sions, the therapist should lengthen the intervals between sessions (Tomm, 1984). Longer intervals indicate progress to clients.

2. The therapist should scurry to beat clients to the door, so to speak. Initiating the termination gives control over it and may well inspire client confidence in the professional's judgment.
3. As clients move toward longer and longer intervals between sessions, the therapist should consider ways to remain available in the future, should a serious problem arise.
4. Once the intervals between sessions become indefinite, the therapist should call or write clients after several months. Not only does this indicate the therapist's continued interest, but also it reminds clients that they have a "family shrink," or someone to call if the old problem recurs or a new problem develops.

Unplanned Terminations

Even the most attentive therapist cannot always foresee terminations that are "planned" by clients. In order to respond intelligently to any form of unplanned termination, the therapist must determine whether the client who decided to terminate therapy was basically satisfied or dissatisfied with the services provided. This determination is best based on direct communication with the client family. Telephone calls made to the person who initiated therapy provide ample information; letters to clients are less successful.

Since clients have the right and ability to decide whether therapy should continue, any excuse for a cancellation or no-show must be accepted with understanding. When the client appears to be satisfied, the therapist should assume that there is a good reason and allow a graceful exit that can be followed by a graceful return for additional sessions whenever the client feels it necessary. Invitations to return for additional sessions should be issued gently and cautiously to avoid the implication that the client needs therapy. Such an implication often meets with automatic defiance. In order to increase the possibility that the client will agree to another session, the therapist may say such things as "I'll be thinking about you. Let me know if you need me."

Dissatisfied clients require a different approach, although it should again be courteous and understanding. Clients who have found their therapist unhelpful decide either that they need another therapist or that therapy, in general, will not help them. Clients who have decided to seek another therapist should be offered an apologetic referral to one. Those who have decided to discontinue therapy altogether, on the other hand, should be congratulated on their decision to do something different and sympathetically encouraged in their efforts. Again, the therapist may ask to be kept informed of the client's progress, but the request may be prefaced with phrases such as "If you get a chance sometime, maybe you'd be willing to. . . ." Such comments leave the door to therapy ajar or at least unlocked.

When clients with serious problems terminate therapy unexpectedly, it is still important to determine whether they are satisfied or dissatisfied with the services provided. The effectiveness of strong advice to return to therapy may depend on the clients' satisfaction with the treatment provided to date. Therapists are often better equipped to deal with hesitant clients than are most physicians. Compliant clients can be directly urged, in the therapist's most professional manner, to continue the prescribed treatment of additional therapy sessions. Defiant clients, or those most likely to resist the advice of authorities, must be approached differently. For example, a therapist may say to a hesitant teen-ager, "Of course, you don't *need* therapy, but we might be able to figure out a way to get your parents and teachers off your back." These varying client attitudes require a flexible approach not practiced by many physicians, but thoroughly described for family therapists by Rohrbaugh, Tennen, Press, White, Raskin, and Pickering (1977).

Serious cases also demand careful management because of the potentially calamitous consequences of becoming known as a professional who can't engage clients who really need help. Referral sources simply do not continue to send clients to those who, for example, let substance abusers quit therapy after two sessions. For this pragmatic reason, therapists who use the medical practice model of termination must either adapt the method adequately to engage serious cases or provide ample explanations for their unconventional treatment method. When all efforts to involve people with serious problems have failed, therapists should try hard to involve other family members in regular sessions. This practice allows the therapist to tell referral sources that he is continuing his efforts to get to the "real" client involved. While clearly not good enough for some sources, this feat is always seen as an honest effort.

CONCLUSION

I have discussed termination with therapists, teachers, and trainers. One of the themes of these discussions has been therapists' personal struggles with the termination process. Some of the therapists' concern is due to their idealized view of what termination should be, but the real struggle has its origins in a more important issue.

Termination—in the usual sense of the word—raises questions about the efficacy of therapy. At the end of a case, it is difficult not to reflect on the success or failure of treatment. Conscientious therapists worry when clients terminate unexpectedly, often saying to themselves, "I wonder what I did wrong." The medical practice model of termination can help to keep terminations in perspective. Therapists must continue to assess the effectiveness of their work, but they must allow clients to leave therapy whenever they wish. The assumption that every unexpected termination is a personal failure discloses a controlling and non-systemic view of therapy that is unhealthy for all concerned, and especially unflattering to those who claim a systemic orientation.

Further implications of the medical practice model of termination are as yet unknown. Like all models, it must be judged according to its usefulness (Harré, 1970), and that will take time.

REFERENCES

Fisch, R., Weakland, J., & Segal, L. (1982). *Tactics of change*. San Francisco: Jossey Bass.

Haley, J. (1967). *Advanced techniques of hypnosis and therapy: Selected papers of Milton H. Erickson, M.D.* New York: Grune & Stratton.

Haley, J. (1976). *Problem solving therapy*. San Francisco: Jossey Bass.

Harré, R. (1970). *The principles of scientific thinking*. Chicago: University of Chicago Press.

Rohrbaugh, M., Tennen, H., Press, S., & White, L. (1981). Compliance, defiance, and therapeutic paradox: Guidelines for strategic use of paradoxical interventions. *American Journal of Orthopsychiatry, 51*, 454–467.

Selvini-Palazzoli, M. (1980). Why a long interval between sessions? The therapeutic control of the family-therapist supra-system. In M. Andolfi & I. Zwerling (Eds.), *Dimensions of family therapy* (pp. 161–176). New York: Guilford Press.

Tomm, K. (1984). One perspective on the Milan systemic approach: Part I. Overview of development, theory, and practice. *Journal of Marital and Family Therapy, 10*, 113–125.

Watzlawick, P. (Ed.) (1984). *The invented reality: How do we know what we believe we know? (Contributions to constructivism)*. New York: Norton.

Watzlawick, P., Weakland, J., & Fisch, R. (1974). *Change: Principles of problem formation and problem resolution*. New York: Norton.

5. The Stages of Structural Family Therapy

Betty M. Karrer and John Schwartzman

Models of therapy, like living organisms, evolve from simple to complex systems. Since its inception the Structural Family Therapy model (Minuchin, 1974) has undergone a series of transformations generated by those who followed, those who expanded, and those who questioned. The model's assumptions and application have been validated for psychosomatic families by Minuchin, Rossman, and Baker (1978), and for substance abuse families by Stanton and Todd (1982). Some authors have enriched the model by presenting its evolution and systemic underpinnings (Umbarger, 1984), while others have contributed a comprehensive review of the model's historical background, its central concepts, and relevance for research and training (Aponte & Van Deusen, 1981). Theorists have facilitated a comparative view by contrasting it with some of the major theoretical models in the field (Hoffman, 1981; Madanes, 1981; & Steinglass, 1978). Key concepts, such as boundary and hierarchy (Wood and Talmon, 1983) and the assessment process (Fishman, 1983), have been clarified. Relevant questions have been raised about the model's limitations with regard to resistance (Hoffman, 1983) and its reinforcement of stereotypic feminine and masculine roles (Hare-Mustin, 1978). The implications of the model for training have also received attention. Montalvo (1973) focused on its implications for live supervision, and recently Colapinto (1982) applied the premises of structural thinking to training and supervision. The model's evolution, as well as its wider contextual implications, have also been comprehensively discussed by Minuchin and Fishman (1981) and Minuchin (1984).

Although the process of movement in therapy has been discussed by many authors, the stages of structural family therapy have been discussed only to illustrate the transition from family therapy to marital therapy (Heard, 1978) and the steps in the hospitalization of disturbed children (Combrinck-Graham, Gursky, and Brendler, 1982). Most recently, Umbarger (1983) described the

We wish to thank Douglas C. Breunlin, for his contributions to the clarification of our concepts, and Rathe Karrer, Richard Schwartz, James Kochalka, and Sylvia Flores for helpful editorial assistance.

staging process as it involves, metaphorically, both a spatial and a temporal domain. Until now, however, this highly refined model of therapy has lacked explication in terms of stages.

SPATIAL AND TEMPORAL DIMENSIONS

Within structural family therapy, form is emphasized. The relationship between form (space) and time (process) is the family dance, those multileveled transactions that define various degrees of proximity and distance. The dance defines the boundaries and, consequently, the family relationships. Colapinto (1982) captured structural therapy's emphasis on spatial metaphors: "It is not enough for the therapist to enlarge the frame so that he can see interactional (even circular) sequences of behavior; what is required is the gestalt perception of the painter, the photographer or the moviemaker" (p. 14).

The emphasis on form results in a corresponding deemphasis on time. Furthermore, structural family therapy is ahistorical, because it is based in part on the assumption that the current context maintains both structure and symptoms. In order to understand the overall framework for change across sessions and set appropriate goals over time, however, the therapist needs a perspective that emphasizes both form and time. In short, the therapist needs to think in terms of stages.

THEORETICAL ASSUMPTIONS OF THE STRUCTURAL FAMILY THERAPY MODEL

Perhaps the most basic assumption in the structural family therapy model is that families are part of an evolving ecology. The many ecological levels of organization and abstraction that affect families include sociocultural beliefs, various social systems, the life cycle stages, and everyday adaptational and random events. Within this ecology, the family is a whole entity in itself, as well as a part of larger systems that have a potentially healing or damaging impact on the family.

Minuchin and Fishman (1981) utilized the term *holon*, which derived from the Greek *holos* (whole) and the suffix *on* (particle or part), (Koestler, 1979) to designate the interrelationship of parts and wholes in systems. Within the family, there are many holons; for example, each family member is not only a whole, but also a part of several subsystems. Each holon is nested within a larger context and inevitably serves as context for another. As a consequence, partial selves of each person are utilized in one holon that are not utilized in another, with many potential selves underutilized. The overall goal of therapy is to introduce complexity and flexibility into the family system by changing the way the various holons interact, thus enabling the family to use the underutilized partial selves and giving the family more options for problem resolution.

The introduction of complementarity as a framework for viewing relationships at various levels of abstraction is one of the most creative aspects of the structural family therapy model. Complementarity concerns the way in which members of a family fit with each other and with their larger context. Colapinto (1982) illustrated the concept in the following example: "Neither the son is intrinsically obnoxious, nor his obnoxiousness is being triggered by his mother. Rather, the son, mother, and father each contribute areas of their selves that complement each other in a consistent pattern" (p. 15). In order to examine relationships from the perspective of complementarity, therapists must shift from a reductionistic world view of individual causality to a systems paradigm of mutually influencing processes.

The therapist establishes a strong relationship by joining the family from various positions of proximity and distance. Joining is not to be viewed as a separate stage, but as an ongoing and interrelated process that nurtures the growth of the therapeutic relationship. By joining and participating in the family's struggle from a close position, the therapist experiences the family's dilemma; by joining from a distant position, the therapist can challenge the family to change.

The therapist creates in-session scenarios in which new transactions can be attempted and unbalances the system by purposeful siding with different members. By pushing the system beyond its threshold of tolerance and requiring it to attempt new modes of interaction, the therapist produces change. Direct strategies are preferred. If the family does not change, the therapist must increase the intensity of pressure on the system.

Above all, the therapist is an expander of contexts; a creator of new realities. Because the therapist is always part of the observed, both influencing and being influenced in interactions with the family, the assumptions made as part of the assessment process are only approximations of reality. Nevertheless, the end result is the creation of a workable reality. Creating a workable reality entails several in-session steps: joining, assessing the problem, setting goals, intervening, reading feedback, and beginning the process of change. The family must be helped to change its perception of itself as a family with problems to a perception of itself as a family with solutions. These parts are not discrete, however, but rather form a tapestry of interrelated threads (Breunlin & Cimmarusti, 1983).

FROM ASSUMPTIONS TO STAGES

The creation of a workable reality, one of the hallmarks of structural family therapy, allows therapists to move quickly and initiate the process of change. Minuchin (1979) creates not one, but several workable realities in an initial interview. Together, these several workable realities constitute a framework for change that can be extended across sessions (Schwartz, Barrett, & Saba, 1984). The framework for change is created by a cycle of observation, conceptualization, intervention, feedback, and higher levels of observation. It connects the workable realities to the stages of treatment.

With such a framework, the therapist can stage structural changes according to those subgroups who are considered primary "actors" in the family's dilemma. At the same time, the therapist can plan a series of subgoals for alternate subgroups, "viewers," who need attention later. As the staging task unfolds, the therapist asks "what if" the actors were more like viewers and the viewers more like actors. As a result, one of the most common first stages of treatment '' to create a context in which the primary actors are held in this position until initial change is attained in the family, at which point they can be retired to become viewers.

Thus, the staging process has three steps. First, based on the workable realities created in session, the therapist realigns actors and viewers in different positions of proximity and distance (the spatial dimension of the staging process). Second, the therapist plans subsequent goals and gives them priorities (in-session temporal dimension of the staging process). Third, the therapist connects the workable realities into an overall framework for change, defining the goals and stages over the course of treatment (across-sessions temporal dimension of the staging process). This process is illustrated in Figure 5-1.

In a videotaped consulting interview to the Southbeach Psychiatric Center in Staten Island, New York (1979), Minuchin illustrated the creation of related workable realities and the staging process that culminated in an overall framework for change.

As the family and consultant prepare to enter the room for the interview, he observes that the mother follows her youngest son and almost enters the bathroom with him. Later in the session, he observes that the father readjusts the oldest son's microphone cord for him. These two events provide him with sufficient information to make initial assumptions about the family's structure. The initial workable reality (i.e., the way the family expresses helpfulness), is subsequently utilized in the staging process.

From these interventions, several positions of proximity and distance emerge among the various members of the family. The mother, as she becomes distant from her husband, becomes overly close with her oldest daughter, who discovers that being close to her mother requires her to assume responsibilities beyond those that correspond to her age and role in the family. The father and the oldest son, the identified patient, are also close. In these interactions, however, the father's helpfulness keeps the young man incompetent so that he acts younger than his age. The second daughter and youngest

Figure 5–1 The Creation of a Framework for Change

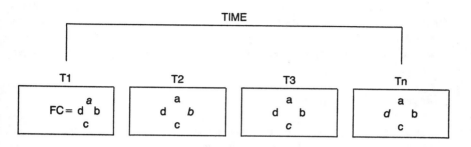

TIME

Time (T1, T2, T3, and Tn) = the temporal dimension within and across sessions.
Framework for Change FC = a,b,c,d, where a,b,c,d are workable realities developed in first session and emphasized across sessions (*a*,b,c,d;*b*,c,d;*c*,d;*d*).

Note: The assumption is made that session 1 (T1) and the last session (Tn) are isomorphic. In reality, between T1 and Tn there is a history that reflects an evolving relationship between the family and the therapist that is increasingly complex. In addition many random events affect the process of treatment over time.

son initially appear as viewers in this dilemma, but they adapt better to the family's struggle by becoming close to or distant from their parents, depending on the context.

Issues of proximity and distance (the actor-viewer metaphor) are further examined in the marital holon. Through the years, the husband and wife have become increasingly detached from each other and unable to maintain the intimacy of their marriage. The increased distance between them accentuates their proximity to their children (mother to daughter and father to son). In an elegant way, Minuchin even links the therapist's helpfulness to the identified patient's ambivalence about staying in the hospital. At the end of the session, it is clear that members of this family oscillate between proximity and distance, between behavior appropriate to their chronological age, and behavior inappropriate to it, and between competence and incompetence.

In this brilliant interview, Minuchin condensed all of therapy into one session. When the session ended, he presented the therapists with several related realities, that should fall into place before the family ends treatment. The therapeutic task is to expand the in-session goals and stages across sessions. For each subsequent session, the therapist should use a workable reality with its appropriate actors and viewers, thus linking the workable realities into an overall framework for change over the entire course of treatment.

THE BROADER TEMPORAL DIMENSION

The transition from one stage to the next is characterized by many fluctuations between transformation and stabilization. Although it may be necessary to address the treatment process as a series of discrete stages for the purposes of communication, it is also necessary to remember the observed oscillations within and between stages.

Stage 1: Searching for Clues

A useful conceptual tool for developing structural assumptions is the notion of isomorphs. Isomorphs in sessions are sequences of short duration (seconds to an hour) that reflect the family's structure, suggest the source of the problem, and indicate those subgroups who are primary actors and viewers in the family's dilemma. Observed in a variety of settings, isomorphs appear and disappear like variations in a musical theme (Breunlin & Schwartz, in preparation).

Once the framework for change has been presented to the family, the task is to select a workable reality from it that the family can accept. Through the use of structural interventions that create in-session intensity, some initial change can usually be achieved with this workable reality. The therapeutic journey has just begun, however. Before lasting change can occur, many such scenarios must be carried out and considerable pressure applied to the family. Over time, the new realities will gradually become part of the family's structure and world view.

Stage 2: Creating New Realities

The creation of new realities that will promote the family's capacity for change requires the therapist to challenge the family's world view, its organization, and its perception of the symptom (Minuchin & Fishman, 1981). Each family member is potentially a door to change. It is not easy to determine which door to use, however, in order to reach the family's underutilized potentialities. Not all members of the family are ready to change at the same time. Some members have more therapeutic momentum at various points than do others. Those who are ready can be utilized to recharge the family's batteries and enact appropriate scenarios. Enacting a scenario in one family holon will, of course, affect the entire family. Thus, the repetition of therapeutic isomorphic transactions across the various holons of the family allows for the gradual expansion of the family's habitual transactions and the creation of new realities.

The therapist can manipulate both space and time in subtle ways. By attempting to make spatial connections between holons that go beyond the habitual patterns of interaction of the family and repeating isomorphic transactions, the therapist can significantly alter the proximity-distance dimension. For example, problem resolution enactments between older and younger siblings, between the women, or between the men in the family can be utilized to connect different family holons in different contexts. Time can also be used in several ways to restructure the family's preferred mode of interaction. Repetition itself is a manipulation of time, because it extends a given content area over a longer time. Extending interactions beyond their preferred threshold of comfort is a restructuring intervention that requires considerable intensity and must be maintained across several sessions so that these new transactional realities become part of the family's habitual pattern of interaction.

The pacing of therapeutic progress varies across families and therapists. Families that are experiencing transitional difficulties will be able to change faster and will, in turn, elicit in their therapists a capacity to promote and activate change. Some families are explorers and will be challenged by the novelty of the territory. Some are careful planners and need to spend more time reviewing their known strengths and their old pathways before venturing into new, unexplored territories. As an agent of change, the therapist's role is to read feedback and lead by following the family's cues (accommodation), as well as to expect the family to follow the therapist's lead (restructuring).

Stage 3: Consolidating Gains

Change always causes some pain, and the therapist who is dealing with the consequences of change must validate that pain. At this time, it is necessary to go beyond the structural family therapy model itself to include self-regulation—not as evidence of pathology, but as a basic aspect of all change—in the model's framework for change. The negative aspects of self-regulation have been highlighted at the expense of its essential role in adaptation. All living systems must regulate themselves in order to maintain their structure. Oscillations between the characteristic range of equilibrium, both positive and negative, allow the organism to maintain balance (Capra, 1982). This is particularly so when there are perturbations in the environment, such as therapy, that require the system to change.

It is assumed in structural family therapy that change produces a self-reinforcing cycle of transformation that motivates families to continue changing on their own and that changes can be consolidated by validating new behaviors and challenging old behaviors through increased intensity. Anticipating the consequences of change by repeating previous strategies and increasing intensity does not always adequately prepare families for the consequences of change, however. The questions of changing directions to deal with the consequences of change and of utilizing the process of self-regulation itself to recreate frameworks for change have been raised by authors who use paradoxical strategies during this stage of treatment (Haley, 1976, 1980, 1983; Madanes, 1981, 1983; Palazzoli, Cecchin, Prata, & Boscolo, 1978; Papp, 1981, 1983; Watzlawick, Weakland, & Fisch,

1974). Minuchin himself has been observed to use paradoxical strategies in his interviews (Hoffman, 1981).

In practice, Minuchin does indeed address the consequences of change. There should be a clear conceptual framework within structural family therapy that acknowledges this need, however. For the present, it is proposed that strategic interventions be introduced to get past this transition.

Stage 4: Ending

Although virtually unaddressed by the structural family therapy model, termination can happen in a number of ways. Ideally, there is a mutual realization that therapy has been successfully completed. Some families present clear indications of success. For example, their rules are explicit, the regulation of information among all subsystems is clear, all family members function at a predominantly age-appropriate level, they show a varied adaptational approach to everyday struggles, and their oscillation between transformation and stability does not require a pervasive symptom. These are all solid goals of structural family therapy, but must they all be attained before therapy can end? How much therapy is enough? Is therapy a vaccination against all trouble, or is it a booster that may need to be administered at later times? Therapy can become a way of life and, in fact, can be a solution that becomes a problem. Given the developmental stage of family therapy as a field, there are no certain cures, only approximations; no vaccines, only boosters.

Once more, it is necessary to go beyond the structural family therapy model and raise some questions as to when therapy should be ended. Schwartz (1983), for example, noted the lack of clear guidelines within structural family therapy for this stage of treatment. The model clearly states that its goal is growth for the entire family. However, who defines how much growth is needed? Although it is important to consider whether the goals in the original framework for change have been met, the therapist's judgment and values ultimately provide the rationale for continuing or terminating treatment.

Preferably, termination is the result of gradual planning, but it is occasionally the result of a sudden realization. When the therapist raises the question of termination, some families voice their belief that the work is done; others attempt to create a reality of helplessness with its complementary reality of helpfulness in the therapist. Most families emerge wiser and with expanded options, however. Whether the termination results from a gradual process, a sudden realization of the need to end, or a seemingly premature decision initiated by the family, it should be a clearly delineated stage that is purposefully utilized in treatment. Planning need not take several sessions, but can effectively take place within the second half of the last session.

Termination as a result of gradual planning can include the following steps: weather the consequences of change, create less in-session intensity, assume a peer-like position, or that of a distant relative who takes an interest in the family, focus on the family's strengths and credit them with therapeutic gains, space sessions, and prescribe vacations (summer or Christmas holiday interludes).

It is important to consider both the spatial and temporal dimensions of the staging process to link the treatment process within and across sessions. The model suggested here utilizes a series of workable realities created in-session, to realign actors and viewers in different positions of proximity and distance. It plans subsequent goals and stages, defining what actors and viewers will be focused at which time. Last, it serves to connect the workable realities into an overall framework for change that connects the goals and stages over the course of treatment.

REFERENCES

Aponte, H.J., & Van Deusen, J. (1981). Structural family therapy. In A.S. Gurman & D.P. Kniskern (Eds.), *Handbook of family therapy* (pp. 310–360). New York: Brunner/Mazel.

Breunlin, D.C., & Cimmarusti, R.A. (1983). Seven opportunities for brief therapy: A recipe for rapid change. In M. Aronson & L. Wolberg (Eds.), *Group and family therapy* (pp. 282–285). New York: Brunner/Mazel.

Breunlin, D.C., & Schwartz, R.C. Sequences: Toward a common denominator of family therapy (in preparation).

Capra, F. (1982). *The turning point*. New York: Simon & Schuster.

Colapinto, J. (1982). Beyond technique: Teaching how to think structurally. *Journal of Strategic and Systemic Therapies, 2,* 12–20.

Combrinck-Graham, L., Gursky, E.J., & Brendler, J. (1982). Hospitalization of single-parent families of disturbed children. *Family Process, 21,* 141–152.

Fishman, H.C. (1983). Reflections on assessment in structural family therapy. In B. Keeney (Ed.), *Diagnosis and assessment in family therapy*. Rockville, Md.: Aspen Systems Corporation.

Haley, J. (1976). *Problem-solving therapy: New strategies for effective family therapy*. San Francisco: Jossey Bass.

Haley, J. (1980). *Leaving home*. New York: McGraw-Hill.

Haley, J. (1984). *Ordeal therapy*. San Francisco: Jossey Bass.

Hare-Mustin, R.J. (1978). A feminist approach to family therapy. *Family Process, 17,* 181–193.

Heard, D.B. (1978). Keith: A case study of structural family therapy. *Family Process, 17,* 339–353.

Hoffman, L. (1981). *Foundations of family therapy*. New York: Basic Books.

Koestler, A. (1979). *Janus: A summing up*. New York: Random House.

Madanes, C. (1981). *Strategic family therapy*. San Francisco: Jossey Bass.

Madanes, C. (1984). *Behind the one way mirror: Advances in the practice of strategic therapy*. San Francisco: Jossey Bass.

Minuchin, S. (1974). *Families and family therapy*. Cambridge, Mass.: Harvard University Press.

Minuchin, S. (1979). *Videotaped consulting interview to the Southbeach Psychiatric Center*. Staten Island, New York.

Minuchin, S. (1984). *The family kaleidoscope*. Cambridge, Mass.: Harvard University Press.

Minuchin, S., & Fishman, H.C. (1981). *Family therapy techniques*. Cambridge, Mass.: Harvard University Press.

Minuchin, S., Rosman, B.L., & Baker, L. (1978). *Psychosomatic families: Anorexia nervosa in context*. Cambridge, Mass.: Harvard University Press.

Montalvo, B. (1973). Aspects of live supervision. *Family Process, 12*, 343–359.

Palazzoli, M.S., Cecchin, G., Prata, G., & Boscolo, L. (1978). *Paradox and counterparadox*. New York: Aronson.

Papp, P. (1983). *The process of change*. New York: Guilford Press.

Schwartz, R.C. (1983). At rainbow's end. *Family Therapy Networker, 7*, 39–40.

Schwartz, R.C., Barrett, M.J., & Saba, G. (1985). Family therapy for bulimia, in D.M. Garner & P.E. Garfinkel (Eds.), *Anorexia nervosa and bulimia*, 280–307. New York: Guilford Press.

Stanton, M.D., & Todd, T. (1982). *The family therapy of drug addiction*. New York: Guilford Press.

Steinglass, P. (1978). The conceptualization of marriage from a systems theory perspective. In T.J. Paolino & B.S. McCrady (Eds.), *Marriage and marital therapy*. New York: Brunner/Mazel.

Umbarger, C.C. (1983). *Structural family therapy: Theory, practice, and technique*. New York: Stratton.

Watzlawick, P., Weakland, J.H., & Fisch, R. (1974). *Change: Principles of problem formation and problem resolution*. New York: W.W. Norton.

Wood, B., & Talmon, M. (1983). Family boundaries in transition: A search for alternatives. *Family Process, 22*, 347–357.

6. The Stages of Strategic Family Therapy

Judith Mazza

Endings are elusive, middles are nowhere to be found, but worst of all is to begin, to begin, to begin.

Donald Barthelme, 1968

Therapists, in collaboration with their clients, organize the interventions used to reach a goal. The first decision every therapist must make is how to begin. A strategic therapist begins therapy by gathering information about the presenting problem. As there is no formula guaranteed to resolve complicated problems, the strategic therapist must select an individualized course of action for each case. The hypotheses, goals, interventions, and postures vary throughout the course of a case. The therapist must move gracefully from one stage of therapy to the next, refocusing attention at the correct time, with the proper people, and in an effective way.

Whether a problem is solved quickly and smoothly, or slowly and unevenly, it makes sense that the therapeutic process that produced the change has followed a pattern similar to that of the change itself. The patterns change throughout the course of the therapy. Thinking of a therapy in stages not only helps the therapist maintain a flexible posture but also indirectly influences the clients' pattern of change.

ISSUES IN STAGING STRATEGIC THERAPY

Because strategic therapy has no set methodology, it cannot be described as a rigid sequence of stages. Early writings in strategic therapy implied that there were occasions on which "Stage B" usually followed "Stage A" (Haley, 1976), but more recent thinking casts doubt even on that assumption. A stage of therapy that once appeared to be part of a predictable sequence may actually be the iatrogenic result of the interventions used. For example, it was once thought that, if one parent of a child with a problem was more peripheral than the other, a marital stage would follow the stage of treatment that focused on the child's problem (Haley, 1976). If, however, the therapist does not use the peripheral parent to break up the intense dyad, but chooses other strategies to solve the child's problems, a marital stage may not be reached. The strategic therapist should consider the therapy finished when the presenting problem is solved. It may not be necessary to explore the parents' private lives after the child's problem is solved. The therapist who intrudes, uninvited, may alienate the parents, thus making it less likely that they will seek therapeutic assistance if problems arise in the future.

Still, if a family member is having difficulty, family life becomes organized around that member's continuing problems. When the symptoms change, family life should change. If the identified patient is a young child and the parents have adjusted to that child's problems, the therapist must find a way to help the parents readjust when the problems have been resolved. This does not imply that marital problems were at the root of the child's problems, but that the parents' adjustments in their lives as a result of the child's problems are no longer necessary.

The stages of a specific therapy may loosely follow the stages that the family has gone through as the problem developed, but in the reverse order. For example, Haley (1980) described the therapeutic approaches used when families have a disturbed member who is at the point of leaving home. When the leaving home problem has included hospitalization of a young adult, the family has often gone through a specific sequence of events prior to the hospitalization:

- The young adult has generally demonstrated some difficult behavior that the family has been unable to control.
- Outpatient therapists have engaged the identified patient in treatment.
- Medication may have been prescribed.
- The problems have continued to escalate, and social control agents (e.g., police, courts) may have become involved.
- Hospitalization appeared to be the only choice.

The strategic therapist begins by undoing that which occurred last. Thus, the first stage is to disengage the family from the hospital staff and from other social control agents. Medication is then reduced and discontinued as the young person improves. The therapist helps the family return to the point at which problems were first experienced. The parents become more involved in guiding the identified patient's daily activities. If the young person was planning to enter the work world before the hospitalization, emphasis would be placed on his finding a job. If he was about to begin college, he would be helped to enroll. If he was about to graduate from school, he would be helped to meet the appropriate requirements. As the young person's life becomes normal, the family's life becomes normal. The therapist helps the parents deal with each other in a more satisfactory way, anticipating the eventual disengagement of the identified patient from the family and the continuation of the family's life cycle.

The notion of stages is more pervasive in strategic therapy than the reversal of sequences that have led to a problem situation. Most applied technical aspects of the therapy can be broken into stages as well.

VARIABLES THAT DEFINE THE STAGE OF THERAPY

A stage of therapy is characterized by the constancy of some aspect of the therapy, but many variables may mark a particular stage. Such variables include the presenting problem, the development of strategies, the directives that are appropriate, the degree of therapist involvement, the establishment of rapport, and the social unit(s) involved in the therapy. Information gathered at the beginning of the therapy may suggest a possible stage of therapy, but it would be an error to assume that families with similar problems would follow the same stages of treatment.

The problem that the therapist and client are attempting to solve is the most important variable. It defines the focus, and all technical aspects of the therapy are influenced by the problem to be solved. Some clients initially seek treatment to solve one problem, but request help with another after the first has been solved. In these cases, the stage of therapy can be labeled according to the problem being solved; the number of problems to be solved determines the number of different stages.

A strategy is the plan that the therapist follows to produce change. In the first stage, the therapist gathers information to set goals for the therapy; this information is the basis for the therapist's initial hypothesis, from which the therapist organizes a tentative strategy. The second stage begins when the therapist prescribes tasks. The third stage addresses the consequences of the changes that occur. The cycle begins again as the therapist gathers new information. Subsequent directives produce further change, which the therapist must take into account when planning the next step.

Everything that a therapist does in relation to a client may be considered a directive (Haley, 1976). Directives or tasks are what the therapist asks the client to do and are a direct reflection of the therapist's approach to solving the problem. Directives change interactions among involved family members, both in and out of the therapy sessions. Haley (1976) wrote that directives have three purposes: to change behavior, to intensify the client's relationship with the therapist, and to gather information. Every directive is given in stages. The therapist gives a directive, observes its effect, and modifies it, if necessary.

In order to influence a client, the therapist must build a relationship with that client—in stages—through the use of language. In the first stage, the therapist uses the client's own words to build rapport. This stage may last a few minutes or several sessions. Once the client has confidence in the therapist's understanding of the problem, the therapist can move to the next stage, which involves introducing a change in the problem definition (relabeling) or a change in the client's frame of reference (reframing). The therapist often gives the newly defined problem a positive connotation and places the symptoms firmly within the client's arena. These redefinitions motivate the clients to do what is necessary to solve the problem. This process is repeated throughout the course of the therapy.

The therapist's level of involvement may distinguish one stage of therapy from the next. Therapists usually involve themselves intensely at the beginning of the therapy and assume a different position as the therapy nears its end (Haley, 1976). Because therapists and clients influence each other, therapists should reevaluate their level of involvement as the clients change. In addition, therapists may change their posture (which may be described in terms such as central, peripheral, light, serious, humorous, powerful, helpless, encouraging, discouraging, logical, or illogical) in order to motivate the family to follow particular directives. Therapists can use their posture to align themselves with one family member or another and, thus, change coalitions and interactions within the family.

A social unit is the group of people considered by the therapist in forming hypotheses and designing strategies. As therapy progresses, the number of people involved in the treatment is likely to change. At times, a treatment unit may be restricted to the nuclear family; at other times, it may be expanded to include the extended family, professionals, neighbors, religious leaders, and others. Such changes in the treatment unit may signal a change in the focus, as well as a change in the stage of therapy.

CASE STUDY: THE DAUGHTER WHO THOUGHT SHE COULD NOT BE A WIFE

Clients rarely follow the scenario written in textbooks, but the following case study demonstrates a variety of stages in the treatment of a suicidal woman. The therapist could not have anticipated that seven stages would be needed, but she remained flexible as the stages emerged and integrated information from one to prepare for the next.

Stage 1: Crisis Intervention

"I don't deserve to live. I should be exterminated!" Barbara said in front of her husband and therapist. Jim appeared frustrated, angry, and hopeless. "I just don't know what to do when she says that," he said. "Did the psychiatrist evolve an emergency plan for you both when Barbara says those things?" the therapist inquired. "No," Jim said. "He won't even speak to me on the phone."

A routine marital therapy consultation had quickly become a crisis interview. The strategic therapist realized that, although Barbara should disengage from her individual therapist, it was more important at this point to ensure that Barbara would not harm herself. An emergency plan was needed. In order to effect such a plan, the therapist needed control of the case. Therefore, it was necessary for the couple to disengage from all other professional helpers; the involvement of more than one therapist increased the risk of confusion and error. The presenting problems were too serious to take that chance.

> Barbara had voluntarily entered a local psychiatric hospital after making two suicidal gestures. She continued to make suicidal comments, however, which frightened and angered her husband. At the time of their initial consultation with the strategic therapist, Barbara had been discharged from the hospital for a month, was in biweekly individual therapy, and was taking antidepressants. They had been referred for marital therapy by the wife's psychiatrist, Dr. L., who had alienated Jim and then refused all contact with him.
>
> Jim and Barbara were in their early 30s and had been married over two years. Both were well educated and held professional positions. Jim had just started a new and rather exciting job. Barbara had enjoyed her job until just before the hospitalization.
>
> Barbara came from a higher class family than did Jim and was the youngest of three children. Her parents had intruded in her marriage on many occasions, and Jim was very bitter toward Barbara's family. He felt that they were largely responsible for the couple's problems. Barbara's father had told Dr. L. that Jim was violent. It was shortly thereafter that Dr. L. refused contact with Jim.

The therapist devised a strategy that included an emergency plan for Barbara and, it was hoped, would result in her disengagement from the psychiatrist. Jim would not allow Barbara to give the strategic therapist permission to speak with Dr. L., because he was afraid that Dr. L. would turn the therapist against him. The therapist agreed not to call for the time being, but only if they would follow the emergency plan exactly as outlined. The plan had several components. Jim was to call Dr. L. every time that Barbara cried uncontrollably and/or made suicidal statements. If Dr. L. was not helpful at those times, they were to do one of three things: call the strategic therapist for an emergency session, plan an activity for the two of them away from the house, or invite friends to visit. Under no circumstances was Barbara to be left alone.

Stage 2: Disengaging Colleagues

The therapist anticipated that, because the psychiatrist had released Barbara from the hospital without an emergency plan and appeared to be afraid of Jim, it was unlikely that he would be helpful during a crisis. The therapist also expected that this lack of response would eventually cause Barbara to discontinue treatment with Dr. L. Taking a clear and strong position in regard to the presenting problems helped the therapist to assume an expert posture and to achieve symmetry with the psychiatrist.

Stage 3: Balancing Power within the Marriage

Barbara gained power in the marriage through her symptoms (i.e., suicide threats and gestures) and through coalitions with her parents and individual therapist. The more power she gained, the more distraught Jim became. If Jim could become instrumental in blocking further hospitalizations and/or suicide gestures, he would be raised in the hierarchy, and power in the marriage would be balanced. To accomplish this, the therapist had to enter into coalitions with Barbara, Jim, and Barbara's parents at appropriate points in the therapy.

The therapist explored the events that precipitated Barbara's hospitalization in order to define the sequence of events that would have to be reversed. Understanding the sequence would allow for the development of a strategy to raise Jim in the hierarchy and block future hospitalizations.

> Jim and Barbara described the months preceding her hospitalization as very stressful. Owing to the interference of her parents in their lives and a series of events in which Jim had been rejected by Barbara's parents, Jim had insisted that Barbara break off contact with them. She had done so in a letter the previous fall. She had many misgivings about the letter, but she wanted to be loyal to her husband. In addition to the extended family problems, her job, once a source of pride and comfort, had become a source of stress and anxiety. Barbara's father had become ill, although he later recovered. Shortly thereafter, she stuck her head in the oven and turned on the gas while Jim watched. They went to a local crisis center, but she bolted from the session. Twenty-four hours later, she admitted herself to the hospital, where she remained for six weeks.

It was now clear that any interventions must involve Barbara's parents. Jim had attempted to dominate Barbara with his grievances and resentments over her parents' interference and rejection of him, over his lack of access to her psychiatrist and the psychiatrist's treatment of him, and over Barbara's subsequent neglect of him as a marital partner.

The therapist put Jim in charge of the renegotiation of Barbara's relationship with her parents, convincing him that the current problems could easily continue unless Barbara resolved her problems with her parents and that she could do so only if she spent blocks of time with them. If Jim took a position that pushed Barbara toward her parents, she would not have to make a choice between her husband and her parents. The therapist told Jim that, because Barbara would rather kill herself than make that choice, he had the opportunity to save her life. No one else could. Jim accepted the challenge and agreed to follow the therapist's instructions, putting his grievances aside to save his wife's life.

Stage 4: Separating from Parents

The focus at this stage of treatment was to find a way for Barbara to separate from her parents without jeopardizing her marriage. Jim had previously attempted to "help" Barbara do this by insisting she break off contact. This had resulted in an escalation of problems for everyone, however. Before relationships could improve, they had to be renegotiated, which necessitated a period of intensification between Barbara and her parents. It was hoped that, if this period of intensification could be maintained long enough, a natural separation would result.

A few sessions later, Barbara reported to the therapist that her parents had decided to sell their home of 30 years and move out of state to be near her older sister and their grandchildren. She felt "left behind" and anxious about the effect of this move on her relationship with her parents. Jim was pleased they were moving farther away and hoped that this alone would resolve the problems.

The psychiatrist continued to be unhelpful, and Barbara stopped seeing him. Barbara continued to make suicidal comments and gestures. Jim followed the therapist's plan and insisted that Barbara help her parents move to their new home. A session was held with Barbara's parents and the young couple to solicit everyone's agreement to this plan. Mr. and Mrs. F., Barbara's parents, indicated to the therapist that, although they had their reservations about Jim, they were generally supportive of the couple's relationship and were willing to do whatever was necessary to help Barbara return to a normal life.

The therapist used Barbara's symptoms to involve her intensively with her parents (Mazza, 1984). The next time that Barbara became suicidal, Jim sent her home to her parents. Her symptoms disappeared within 24 hours. During this stage of therapy, this strategy was repeated three or four times. Jim was encouraged to restrain her from returning too quickly; moreover, by insisting that Barbara spend time with her parents, Jim was allowing Barbara to be both wife and daughter simultaneously.

The therapist wrote Barbara and her parents a letter to promote certain discussions between them. As Mr. and Mrs. F. had been very involved in the couple's marriage, it was assumed that they would not discontinue their involvement immediately. Because they would need a more reasonable way of staying involved, they were asked to serve as consultants to both Barbara and Jim in the event of future crises. As Barbara had decided to seek new employment, Mr. and Mrs. F. were asked to help her find new purpose in her life. They were asked to use their success in negotiating a new "retired" life as an example for her.

Barbara returned to Jim after a month's separation. She reported that she was happy to come home and appeared much less depressed. She knew that her home was no longer with her parents, and she saw that she could occupy a role as their daughter, even though they were hundreds of miles away.

She engaged in an intensive and successful job search. The almost constant threats of separation that had been vehemently expressed during their arguments disappeared. As Barbara began living more normally, Jim began to experience increased problems.

The couple was asked to communicate by letter, as well as by telephone. The letter writing, a courtship ritual from their past, was the beginning of the renewal of the relationship between Jim and Barbara.

Stage 5: Leaving the Past Behind

The therapist never learned precisely what had happened between Barbara and her parents. Because her suicidal symptoms disappeared after increased contact with them and because she was ready to find new employment on her return home, however, the therapist concluded that her parents need no longer be included in the therapy and that Barbara and Jim could focus on their relationship. With this change in focus, the treatment unit changed. The therapist planned her strategy as if she was beginning a new therapy.

Jim had been experiencing digestive problems and some sleep disturbance. He complained that everything had been done for Barbara, nothing for him. He woke up early in the mornings and berated Barbara, saying that she was responsible for the injustices of the past and that she had neglected him as a wife. Barbara appeared helpless during his onslaughts. She knew he had helped her with her parents, and she wanted to help him. Part of her problem was that anything she attempted to do was treated by Jim as "too little, too late."

The therapist told Jim and Barbara that a terrible imbalance had developed in their relationship over the years. This imbalance was due to the fact that Jim was expert in "giving," but did not know how to "receive" with grace and good cheer. Jim brightened considerably. He said that the therapist was correct and that this problem had begun when he was a child. His birthday occurred right after Christmas, and he had always felt short-changed. He would cover this up by acting as if it were not important, but he never felt comfortable when people tried to make him feel special.

In Jim's presence, Barbara was instructed that, as a wife, she would have to help her husband over this problem, or the imbalance in their relationship would never be corrected. Her success would be marked by a gradual reduction in the morning harangues, but she should be prepared for Jim's ingratitude. Jim was told that he would probably not appreciate Barbara's efforts and would probably continue to make it difficult for her to be giving toward him. These emotional responses would dissipate gradually. When he was ready, and it might happen suddenly, he would be able to enjoy his wife fully.

The paradoxical instigations for both partners made this stage of therapy different from the previous one (Haley, 1984). The intervention was an ordeal for Barbara in that she had to continue to be giving and generous to Jim, despite his rude manner and morning harangues. The therapist selected an ordeal as the intervention for a number of reasons. It appeared that Jim had designed his own ordeal for Barbara. The morning harangues were odious to both; they began their day with an argument and often continued it in the evening. The therapist felt that allowing Barbara's ordeal to continue—but under the therapist's control—would have beneficial side-effects for the couple. The ordeal would intensify their commitment to each other. If the therapist was harder on them than they were on each other, it was hoped that they would form a stronger coalition (possibly against the therapist) and begin to disengage from the therapy.

Barbara reluctantly did as she was asked. She cooked Jim more interesting meals, increased the frequency of love-making, and planned a Caribbean vacation just before she began her new job. The vacation was paid for from a special savings account in Barbara's name. She gave Jim the remainder of the money to spend as he chose. He decided that he would get the most satisfaction from placing it in their retirement fund. Jim gradually softened and became more appreciative. The morning harangues gradually ceased, replaced by cuddling and love-making. They both reported that their relationship continued to improve.

Stage 6: Beginning to Disengage from Treatment

The therapist decreased the frequency of sessions and recessed the therapy for the summer. Jim and Barbara had been in treatment for approximately 12 months. Toward the end of the summer, the therapist received a distraught telephone call from Jim. They were having difficulties again and requested an appointment.

Jim and Barbara told the therapist that their difficulties once again involved their relationship with Barbara's parents. They were invited to visit her parents during the coming holiday season and were frightened that Barbara might have a recurrence of her problems. They discussed possible options, and Jim was put in charge of making the final decision. He appeared to be relieved and made the arrangements.

With a significant decrease in the intensity of therapy, a new stage of therapy had begun. The couple did not need regular appointments, and their relationship did not appear to be in jeopardy. Jim and Barbara would have one more crisis before they could truly disengage from treatment, however.

Stage 7: The Final Disengagement

Jim called the therapist and requested an emergency appointment. Mr. and Mrs. F. were making monthly visits from their retirement home to Jim and Barbara. Although the visits had gone reasonably well, one problem remained. Jim had asked that Mrs. F. apologize to him for the snubs and insults of the past. Her unwillingness to do so especially bothered him because, every time she came to visit, the couple voluntarily gave up their bedroom. Jim felt usurped in his own home.

Jim and Barbara decided that, if she did not apologize, they would wrest control of the visits. They would invite themselves to visit Mr. and Mrs. F., just as Mr. and Mrs. F. invited themselves to visit Jim and Barbara. They would invite themselves at their convenience and might not be available when Mr. and Mrs. F. planned to visit. They laughed and looked forward to the intrigue.

Just as Jim and Barbara were about to send Mr. and Mrs. F. a telegram to announce their unexpected visit, Mrs. F. wrote a contrite letter of apology to Jim! She said that she was "set in her ways" and was sorry for any pain she had caused him. Jim was so pleased that he sent her flowers the following week. Jim and Barbara went away for the weekend. They said, for the first time, the past was truly behind them. They looked forward with renewed enthusiasm to their future together.

Jim and Barbara had solved this last crisis on their own. Neither partner had threatened separation or blamed the other for their dilemma. They evolved their own plan to deal with a difficult (and somewhat recalcitrant) mother-in-law. They recognized that Mrs. F. had her failings. They also felt that they were free to visit or not to visit Barbara's parents. Barbara could love and maintain a relationship with her parents and husband at the same time. Although Jim and Barbara could have periodic crises, it was clear that they had moved to a new stage of their marriage.

CONCLUSION

In providing therapy for Jim and Barbara, the therapist had worked to "undo" the steps that Barbara and Jim had gone through, in the reverse order. The first stage was to protect Barbara's life and then disengage the couple from other professional colleagues. As this was being done, the therapist balanced the couple's relationship, which provided a base to help Barbara separate from her parents. Once the separation was accomplished, the couple needed a way to put the past to rest, which then permitted them to regulate distance and closeness with extended family. In the final stage of treatment, the couple disengaged from the therapist by solving a crisis in their own style.

The therapist used the information gathered in each stage to anticipate and plan for the next stage of treatment. The sequence of stages was specifically tailored to the couple's situation. Each stage had a slightly different focus and used different interventions. As the treatment progressed, the social unit changed from the couple alone, to the couple with extended family, and then the couple alone. The therapist was intensively involved with both partners in the beginning of treatment. As Barbara and Jim's relationship improved, the therapist pulled away, permitting them to solve the last crisis on their own.

There is never one and only one way to solve a problem. Even therapists working in similar ways will employ different strategies. This diversity is encouraged in a strategic approach, because it is expected that therapy will be tailored to individual situations. Strategic therapy encourages creativity on the part of therapists, as each combines personal experience and professional training to solve a client's specific dilemma.

REFERENCES

Haley, J. (1973). *Uncommon therapy: The psychiatric techniques of Milton H. Erickson, M.D.* New York: W.W. Norton.

Haley J. (1976). *Problem-solving therapy.* San Francisco: Jossey Bass.

Haley, J. (1980). *Leaving home: The therapy of disturbed young people.* New York: McGraw-Hill.

Haley, J. (1984). *Ordeal therapy.* San Francisco: Jossey Bass.

Mazza, J. (1984). Symptom utilization in strategic therapy. *Family Process, 23*(4), 487–500.

7. Stages of Family Therapy with Divorcing Families

Virginia A. Simons and Douglas H. Sprenkle

The crisis of divorce can overwhelm a family. There are few prescribed behaviors, rites, or precedents for the family that is proceeding through separation and divorce. Working with families during this transition can place intense demands on a therapist, both conceptually and operationally.

A PERSPECTIVE

The structure of divorcing families varies greatly, depending on four factors: (1) the particular characteristics of the family system prior to the initiation of divorce proceedings, (2) current familial interactions, (3) the sequencing of events in the divorcing process, and (4) the larger context of the family. Several structural options are available, such as a joint hierarchical organization between the ex-spouses with mutual sharing of the children or sole custody with one primary parent and an involved and vigilant visiting parent, a less involved (but available) noncustodial parent, or an absent parent. The success of each of these arrangements depends on different conditions. For example, joint custody arrangements seem to be successful only when the parents have voluntarily chosen to participate, the family members show a high degree of flexibility, and the parents are able to separate child-rearing from marital failure (Ahrons, 1981; Goldsmith, 1982; Steinman, 1981). Shared parenting is contraindicated when there is court involvement, when either parent reports extreme guilt, or when there is a great deal of conflict between the parents (Irving, Benjamin, & Trocine, 1984).

The reactions of a family to the transitions of divorce depend heavily on what has occurred prior to the divorce decision, the way in which the parents are coping, the functioning of the sibling subsystem, and the strengths of each family member. Divorce weakens the protective boundaries of the family, not only because the parental subsystem is strained and often conflicted, but also because all relation-

V. Simons thanks the staff of the Families of Divorce Project for stimulating some of the ideas presented.

ships within the family are changing simultaneously. It challenges hierarchical boundaries within the family and forces members to reconsider their alliances. Children feel loyalty pulls and may actively choose sides; a parent may disclaim the other's effectiveness and make erratic judgments. Parents may confuse the failure of the spousal relationship with failure of the parent-child relationship, or each may see the other's parenting as a failure. Children, out of anxiety and fear, may also confuse issues, worrying that they will be rejected because of the parental divorce or that they will have to choose sides and thus reject a parent or a sibling. The outcome is more likely to be positive if the family members can communicate, think toward the future, and tolerate differences.

The complicated process of sequencing, or the "timing" of events during divorce, is important for adaptive reorganization. Events that move the family to an alternate structure are defined by, and can be stimulated from, a series of psychological and logistical shifts in hierarchy, proximity, and family roles. A family member who clings to past patterns of the old system or who rushes head-long into new relationships and new styles of interrelating influences the eventual outcome of the reorganization and creates confusion for the children (Montalvo, 1982). Sequencing is also affected by the perceptions that each parent holds about his or her role and the future of all familial relationships, as well as by the changes that occur in these perceptions over time. A recently separated parent may shun the other parent, for example, attempting to take on all responsibility for decisions regarding the children. These attitudes and perceptions may become more flexible, however, as the full meaning of that responsibility becomes clear.

The experiences and perceptions of children in the divorce process are different from those of their parents. Wallerstein and Kelly (1980) found that, even when their parents had been caught in severely unhappy marriages, the children did not usually want them to divorce. Although the parents, especially the mothers, appear to recover more rapidly and completely from the divorce than the children do (Wallerstein & Kelly, 1980), the quality of parenting diminishes, at least temporarily, during the crisis of divorce. Frequently, children long for reparative time alone with one parent, but the parent insists on overprogramming the children's activities or on rushing them into new relationships and unfamiliar situations. Other children make changes more quickly than does the parent. Finally, parental conflict has a negative effect on postdivorce parental cooperativeness and on the recovery of children (Ahrons, 1981; Goldsmith, 1982; Heatherington, Cox, & Cox, 1979; Luepnitz, 1983; Wallerstein & Kelly, 1980).

The broader context of each family has a powerful impact during this transition as well. Because the protective boundaries around the family are more easily permeated during divorce, external stresses and influences are more easily felt. Legal proceedings, religious beliefs, cultural backgrounds, economic ramifications, and relationships with extended families can ease, impede, or disrupt the process of divorce.

A FRAMEWORK FOR THE DIVORCING FAMILY

When the therapist uses a holon analysis (Minuchin & Fishman, 1981), the marital holon, the parental holon, the parent-child holon, and the sibling holon all merit careful attention at some time in the therapeutic process. Throughout the stages of divorce, the therapist determines the consideration given to particular holons at various times. Once a decision to divorce has been made, attention shifts from the marital holon to the parental holon; once separation has occurred, the parent-child and sibling holons quickly gain consideration.

Most children cannot afford extended periods of time without adequate nurturing by their parents. The diminished parenting that takes place during the crisis of divorce can set a pattern that becomes part of the reorganized structure (Abelsohn, 1983; Montalvo, 1982; Wallerstein & Kelly, 1980). Therefore, once the parents have decided to divorce, initial treatment deals primarily with the children's needs and only secondarily with parental issues. Parenting is the one area of functioning that will continue after the spouses divorce. Since the relationships within the post-divorce family are a key factor in the recovery of children, neglect of these dynamics is likely to result in symptoms.

Increasing parental awareness of the children's needs can bring parents relief from their own conflicts as a couple and draw their attention to an arena where they can reorganize more promptly without necessarily experiencing a sense of failure. Efforts to establish common ground regarding the care of the children provide an opportunity to declare different boundaries and encourage adaptation for a more functional, co-parental system (Ahrons, 1981; Goldsmith, 1982). This focus on the children gives the therapist leverage to help the family move toward a new system in which the parents continue parental responsibilities while differentiating their relationship from their spouse. As parents mobilize around the children and see the results of their work, they can feel more confident of their own recovery as well.

Although the care of the children is a place to begin reorganization, it should not take precedence if there are more pressing clinical issues, such as serious depression, psychosis, or other pathological dysfunctions, that must be addressed. In general, however, once the patterns of child care have been established, the parents' individual issues can come to the forefront of treatment.

GENERAL PRINCIPLES

There are several principles that allow therapists optimal movement and perspective, but they are not equally relevant at any given time. Instead, their importance varies as therapy progresses from stage to stage.

Access to All Family Members

Regardless of who contacts the therapist initially, it is essential for the therapist to obtain permission for access to all family members at the outset. It is not necessary for all family members to sit down together during treatment sessions, but this should be an option. This treatment flexibility (i.e., seeing individuals, family subsystems, or the entire family network) serves as a model for flexibility in the postdivorce family. One of the most successful ways for the therapist to gain access to both spouses is to take the initiative by explaining the context of treatment and contacting the other parent. This approach allows for open discussion of the pending therapeutic contract.

Neutrality

Parents who are divorcing have different perspectives, and both are usually convinced that they are right. As the therapist expresses his or her intention to remain neutral, the family tests that neutrality in both subtle and overt ways. Being sensitive to and periodically exploring each parent's views of the therapist's neutrality can prevent loss of one parent in treatment. When temporarily unbalancing the parental subsystem, the therapist must be extremely careful to ensure that neutrality can be regained. Children caught up in loyalty conflicts are keenly aware of the therapist's neutrality and may even mention it as a concern.

Parents often expect specific attitudes in therapists. If, for example, the father expects the therapist to find fault with the mother, changing him or his relationship with the children may not meet his expectations of therapy. Instead, he may feel criticized.

Physical and Legal Requirements

The therapist must take into account the physical arrangements and the legal definitions under which the family is living. For example, some parents may insist that they are "separated," but continue to live in the same household. Treating these parents as if they are separated, when there is no physical separation, encourages a myth and prolongs the stalemate. The therapist, then, contributes to the double reality defined by the family. In other cases, the legality of access to all family members may be a real issue. If the children are in the legal custody of one parent, that parent must give written permission for the noncustodial parent to be involved in treatment with the children, as well as for the children to be involved in treatment. Geographical distance sometimes limits the types of involvement that family members have with each other and in treatment. If the therapist feels it is important to include the distant family members, however, some effort should be made.

The legal process greatly influences parents during separation and divorce, and it can be intricately intertwined with economic and psychological issues. The legalities of a divorce can delay, disrupt, or at times facilitate therapeutic movement. Of utmost importance is access to legal information, such as the kind and type of attorney involvement, court dates, and the current legal issues. At the same time, therapists should clearly state their positions regarding involvement with the legal system as part of a written therapeutic contract. Although most clinicians choose to provide treatment without the involvement of the attorney and the court system, there are times when it is appropriate to discuss certain issues with an attorney or to include the attorneys for a specific part of treatment (Bernstein, 1979).

A family may organize itself solely around the attorney's advice or around the next step in the legal process. Even children may come to depend on the court system to "rescue" them from the stalemates that occur between parents. Because of its adversarial nature, however, the legal process can embroil parents in arguments and freeze the progress of treatment. On the other hand, parents may intelligently weigh the importance of the legal issues against the importance of the psychological issues and decide for themselves the extent of influence that attorneys or court dates will have on them. Therapists may decide to stop therapy until court procedures have been completed, or they may decide that all litigation should be delayed until some point in treatment. Therapists may even seek training in the new discipline of family mediation described by Coogler (1978), Haynes (1981), and Irving (1980).

Tolerance of Emotionality

Intense emotions are to be expected when people divorce. If these emotions exceed a tolerable threshold, however, they can interfere with treatment. Therefore, it is sometimes necessary for the therapist to contain the level of emotions by actively structuring interactions both in and out of sessions. In such a case, the therapist should become direct, even commanding. In order to mediate tension or hostility during sessions, the family therapist may have all communication directed to and from him or her, rather than from parent to parent. The therapist may restrict the discussion between parents to only a specific issue that each parent wants resolved. Time-limited discussions also decrease tension and maintain the focus on problem resolution. The therapist may help the parents to contain their emotions outside sessions by helping them plan an agreement, eliciting a commitment to that agreement from them, and monitoring the effect of the agreement. Through careful planning and compromising, parents can arrange to have their discussions and arguments out of earshot of the children. As a result, conflicts can become more direct, and the couple's style of conflict resolution can be dealt with more easily.

The therapist must plan carefully before seeing extremely conflicted couples. It may be helpful to challenge each one separately in order to determine what might enrage or antagonize him or her during a joint session. Part of therapy involves helping parents learn to contain their conflict long enough to resolve their differences. The therapist must shift the parental emphasis from the spousal conflict to the protection and care of the children. There are times, however, when the hostility between the parents is so explosive that joint sessions are not constructive, and it is necessary to see these spouses or former spouses separately. Conflict is not unusual during divorce; the problem is the extent to which dysfunctional family patterns are created to cope with that conflict and the potential negative effects of the conflict on the children (Luepnitz, 1983; Steinman, 1981; Wallerstein & Kelly, 1980).

Transitional vs. Chronic Problems

Reorganization problems may develop just prior to separation and continue throughout the first 18 to 24 months after separation. It is conceptually and diagnostically important to differentiate the transitional difficulties that arise in the early stages of divorce crises from the more chronic dysfunctional patterns that have been set over a long period of time. The initial stages of transition, when family relationships are shifting and changing chaotically, are the most optimal times for effective and efficient family treatment and preventive work. Interventions at these times often show immediate results, resolving the conflicts and moving the family patterns toward more adaptive styles. Boundary reformation is a critical part of the initial stages of transition; if roles or family patterns have not been adapted to new situations, family pathology can develop (Abelsohn, 1983; Isaacs, 1981). If the family has a symptomatic member or is seeking family treatment more than two or three years after the divorce, postdivorce chronic dysfunctional patterns have probably developed. The balance between the new and the old system, with periodic complementary shifts within the psychological-emotional arena or the legal arena that relate chronologically, allows the family to cope with the new system as it evolves.

STAGES OF DIVORCE TREATMENT

First Stage: Phases of Marital Dissolution

In the first stage of divorce treatment, marital work centers on the decision to separate and/or to divorce. During this phase, one or both spouses think about the possibility of divorce and its ramifications, but neither has made an irrevocable decision. Storm and Sprenkle (1982) noted that conjoint therapy should be emphasized in the decision-making phase. Children should typically be involved only if they are aware of the parents' struggle and are affected by it.

Once a firm decision to divorce has been made by one of the spouses, as evidenced by such acts as obtaining an attorney, exploring alternative housing, or setting a deadline date for physical separation, the children must be considered and involved. During this phase of planning for the separation, both preventive counseling and treatment of presenting problems may be needed. This is when parents begin to recognize that they are divorcing their spouse—not their children—and when the therapist examines the patterns of the family (with any underlying agendas) to determine whether these patterns could interfere in the overall divorce process.

Parents living together are seen together initially, but it may be necessary to see each separately in order to challenge particular stalemates, to give extra support to either parent or both, or to heighten sensitivities to the children that one or the other parent lacks. The children may need separate sessions as well as sessions with their parents. Children are protective not only of themselves, but also of their parents during this stage and may not disclose their areas of pain in the presence of their parents. When seen individually and questioned sensitively, however, most children either demonstrate or discuss openly their anxieties and the particular difficulties in their lives. Seeing siblings together without either of the parents also helps to build stronger alliances and resolve conflicts among them (Eno, 1985).

During the stage of dissolution, therapy can take on a crisis intervention style, in which intense work is directed toward solving particular problems. One marathon session may be all that is needed, or sessions may take place on a frequent basis. Naturally, it is important to see what changes the family can manage on their own, but the therapist must make clinical judgments about when to contain emotions and conflicts, when to use directives, and when to decrease the frequency of sessions.

After the decision to divorce has been made, the first tasks are planning for physical separation and making arrangements for each parent's access to the children. Physical separation should be expedited, because prolonged discussion of separation without physical separation can become extremely stressful for all family members. The period surrounding physical separation evokes emotions and tensions that can run extremely high, and the effort to get through a day without confrontations when physical separation has not yet occurred can take most of the family's energy. The therapist must challenge the parent who is unwilling to relinquish his or her claim to the same household and facilitate that parent's decision to move. Specific, concrete plans regarding housing, financial arrangements, legal arrangements, and child custody must be made. The planning of the physical separation, including the division of the household or other concrete possessions, underscores the breaking of the marital bonds (Schulman, 1981).

The therapist should see the children in order to help them accept and adjust to the divorce. In helping the parents tell the children about the pending divorce, reassuring them of their parents' continued interest, and preparing them for what is to follow, the therapist can help the parents to monitor the children's reactions and abilities to cope with the separation. Parents need to be encouraged to pay particular attention to each child's personal and developmental needs, and they should be forewarned about the numerous and repeated questions that the children may ask. Parents may consider the co-parenting effort paradoxical, however, because of the simultaneous marital separation.

During this phase of treatment, children can be allowed some active role in the separation. Children are interested in which parent they are going to live with, what their access to the other parent will be, if they will have their own rooms, if they will lose friendships or transfer schools, and, in general, what their new life will be like. At this time, the therapist helps the parents to disclose appropriate information to the children and to keep the balance between the past and the future as the two distinct subsystems begin to take form. Parents can involve children in planning by means of (1) conducting "trial runs," such as long weekends or weeks with one parent; (2) learning to enjoy everyday things and activities with the children; (3) allowing the children to participate in the household move in a manner appropriate to their ages; (4) making plans with the children, such as what to do in the new home, how to decorate it, and who stays where.

During and immediately following separation, the therapist must watch for signs that a child is becoming involved in dysfunctional patterns between the parents. A 9-year-old boy who identifies with his father may attempt to keep the family together even for "discipline's" sake by challenging his mother's authority. A 13-year-old girl, sympathetic to her mother, may become overinvolved in her mother's difficulties and be unable to separate appropriately as an adolescent. A parent who feels guilty and depressed may allow the children to be rejecting, critical, or manipulative during the period of separation and thus undermine the hierarchical boundaries of the family in the postseparation adjustment. The therapist must strengthen generational boundaries and help parents to establish appropriate relationships between the child and each parent. For example, a depressed parent may need some individual attention in order to deal with his or her particular guilt or depression and to strengthen his or her executive functioning regarding the children.

Just before and after separation, adults are likely to feel ambivalence, depression, guilt, and anger (Price-Bonham, Wright, & Pittman, 1983). Because they are experiencing a crisis, divorcing parents frequently have limited vision about their alternatives and anything unexpected can agitate, devastate, or enrage them. Treatment should address potential problems that may come up and ways to deal with those problems. It may take time to deal with the individual needs that interfere in the divorce process, but unless the overall therapeutic focus remains on the ongoing process and progress of the separation, family work may get derailed.

Difficulties may arise at this stage of divorce transition as the spouses move through the process at different rates. One parent may be more adamant about the divorce or the progress of separation than the other, or the spouses may alternate being adamant. For example, the mother may be adamant about the divorce initially and become impatient with the father, who is refusing to leave the household; as the father decides to move out of the household, however, the mother may become unreasonable about the father's access to the children, attempt to undermine his attachment to them, and stall his move. These cyclical spurts of change and stalemate may confuse the children, and the therapist may be required to moderate the transition in order to ease the family into new stages and help the parents buffer the children against abrupt or extreme changes.

When there is a great deal of confusion, both the internal and the external boundaries of the family become permeable, resulting in chaos. If the family has little flexibility or adaptability, however, problems can also develop. Learning ways to obtain new and appropriate support for all family members without allowing the intrusion of extended family members, well-meaning neighbors, or the lawyers into the family network is part of the work of the family in this stage (Luepnitz, 1983; Messinger & Walker, 1981).

Second Stage: Phases of Recovery

Recovery work begins immediately after physical separation and encompasses three successive phases of adaptation for families: (1) differentiation, (2) reintegration, and (3) readjustment.

Differentiation

After the new arrangement of the family has been planned, each parent must differentiate his or her own parenting skills and individual issues from those of the other parent. The therapist may see each parent separately with the children in order to begin work on separate parent-child subsystems. The goal during this phase is to establish separate, but cooperative, parenting, in which each parent is providing the most competent care possible for the children and is beginning some individual growth. During this stage, the parents begin to realize fully the impact of their ongoing roles, including new jobs, new lives, and a different style of parenting. The therapist should also help the children as they experience the reality of these changes.

During postseparation, the stresses on the custodial parent differ from those on the noncustodial parent. The custodial parent may feel overwhelmed, depressed, enraged, or bitter about the new responsibilities of caring for the children as a single parent (Weiss, 1979). As a result, the custodial parent may refuse any assistance, or even contact, with the noncustodial parent, which increases his or her stress and distresses the children. Although there is a transitional period for gaining some differentiation and self-confidence as a single parent, there is a danger that the custodial parent will become rigid and the system will become dysfunctional. On the other hand, the noncustodial parent may feel displaced and, in turn, may withdraw and isolate himself or herself from the family, blaming the custodial parent for this isolation. The primary work during this stage is for the noncustodial parent to maintain contact and to develop a parental relationship with the children, even though there may be severe time constraints.

Treatment often focuses on what can be done within the constraints of the quality of the parents' relationship and time availability. For some parents, accepting their inability to "control" much of the other parent's behavior can become an issue. By focusing on the children's needs, parents can moderate the "rushing" or the arrest in parental adjustment. During the phase of differentiation, parents are rarely seen together. They are brought together only for specific, goal-directed work around parenting functions and communications about the children.

Reintegration

At some point, parents must begin to consider their joint roles and functions in the growth and development of the children. Spontaneous signs of reintegration, such as the maintenance of certain routines and rituals or responses to special events, may appear. The therapist may become reinvolved with a family as each subsystem attempts to establish routines or requests specific help in the planning of a special event. Some families contact the therapist for the first time after experiencing difficulty with one or more special event.

As the parents separate and begin to move into divorced family patterns, they should keep as much continuity as possible for the children by maintaining the children's friendships, relationships with extended family members, and routine access to the other parent. Frequently, the children themselves suggest the continuation of certain family routines, such as a family activity night, a regular Sunday brunch with the extended family, or bedtime routines. In order to convey a sense of stability and continuity to adolescents, both parents must set basic limits and structures. Otherwise, adolescents draw comparisons, increase their testing of limits, and may even become combative toward one or both parents.

During reintegration, it is helpful if the parents can cooperate around special events, such as a first communion, a first holiday season, or the first summer vacation. As the parents meet these variances in the routine schedule by means of cooperative planning, the children learn how their parents will cope in the future and begin to understand what their future family network can be. The plans for special events should be made carefully to avoid potential "explosions" between parents that would make the children uncomfortable or embarrass them. The goal is to reassure the children that, although the parents are divorced, they are still available for special celebrations and can cooperate to make the event as special as possible.

Readjustment

Certain events, such as remarriage of one or both parents, relocation of one parent to another geographical area, the increased absence of the noncustodial parent, or a change of residence for one or all of the children, necessitate major readjustments in the relationships of the divorced family members. Past dysfunctional patterns may resurface, or new dysfunctional patterns may develop. Old conflictual patterns that have remained submerged for years may reappear because of the intensity of emotions felt as a major event approaches or as an aftermath of such an event (Hansen, 1982; Sager, Brown, Crohn, Engel, Rodstein, & Walker, 1983). During this phase, families again must renegotiate family roles, relationships, and proximity. Unanticipated problems develop from inadequate planning and constricted patterns of interactions. Families usually enter treatment after the event that necessitates readjustment has occurred, although it is best to work with these families before the event.

Family subgroups that have functioned well during previous phases may feel disparaged when one of the parents remarries. Not only must the system expand to include a step-parent and perhaps step-siblings, but also major adjustments must be made in relationships, especially regarding proximity, power, and alliances. Remarriage can also raise new questions regarding previous custodial decisions. The relocation of a parent may also have serious ramifications for a family, because it usually reduces the frequency of visitation and the visiting parent's input into the children's lives. Children may develop symptoms of loss and grief when the visits of the noncustodial parent become less frequent, especially as the children enter new developmental stages and struggle with new understandings about the absence of one parent (Wallerstein, 1983). Families of divorce must also readjust when there is a change in residence for a child or all children, whether this change is made because of custody renegotiations or litigation, developmental and psychological needs of the children recognized and anticipated by the family, or symptoms in a family subsystem.

The therapist should see various family subsystems during the readjustment stage in order to determine whether the issues involve custody, visitation, or the relationship of the two family subsystems.

One father who had legal joint custody and had seen his children every weekend for two years brought the children to therapy because of difficulties he was having with the children's behavior while they were with him. The therapist contacted the mother, who gave permission for the children's treatment and agreed to remain in telephone contact with the therapist. The mother had been involved in individual treatment and did not feel she was having difficulties with the children. During the initial session, the father acknowledged that he was finding it difficult to manage the children during visits, but he continually blamed his ex-wife for these problems. Because his current problem was really a parenting issue, he was told that the mother would not be included in treatment, but that therapy could proceed with the focus on improving his relationship with his children.

After four sessions, both the father and the children had begun to relate to each other more effectively and had worked out their own set of rules and expectations. The father's relationship with the children required him to accommodate to their growth and development, as well as to adjust to the loss of his girlfriend. The mother spontaneously called the therapist, stating that the children were returning from visits to their father in a better frame of mind and that she was pleased with his weekend care. As the father gained confidence and competence, he began to communicate and share information with his ex-wife openly for the first time.

Families that enter treatment during these later phases are usually motivated by symptoms in one or more of the children or by problems that have resurfaced as a result of a significant event. Therapeutic difficulties during this second stage tend to occur when families are frozen in old patterns that do not allow members to move into more adaptive interactions with each other or with their environment and thus keep them from completing the overall process of divorce.

REFERENCES

Abelsohn, D. (1983). Dealing with the abdication dynamic in the post divorce family: A context for adolescent crisis. *Family Process, 22,* 359–383.

Ahrons, C.R. (1981). The continuing coparental relationship between divorced spouses. *American Journal of Orthopsychiatry, 51*(3), 415–428.

Bernstein, B.E. (1979). Lawyer and therapist as an interdisciplinary team. *Journal of Marital and Family Therapy, 5,* 93–100.

Coogler, O.J. (1978). *Structured mediation in divorce settlement.* Lexington, Mass.: Lexington Books.

Eno, M. (1985). Relationships in families of divorce. In D. Sprenkle (Ed.), *Divorce therapy.* New York: Haworth Press.

Goldsmith, J. (1982). The post divorce family system. In F. Walsh (Ed.), *Normal family process.* New York: Guilford Press.

Hansen, J.C. (1982). *Therapy with remarriage families.* Rockville, Md.: Aspen Systems Corporation.

Haynes, J.M. (1981). *Divorce mediation: A practical guide for therapists and counselors.* New York: Springer.

Heatherington, E.M., Cox, M., & Cox, R. (1979). The family interaction and the social, emotional and cognitive development of children following divorce. In V.C. Vaughn & T.B. Brazelton (Eds.), *The family: Setting priorities.* New York: Science and Medicine Publishers.

Irving, H.H. (1980). *Divorce mediation: A rational alternative to the adversary system.* New York: Universe Books.

Irving, H.H., Benjamin, M., & Trocine, N. (1984). Shared parenting: An empirical analysis utilizing a large data base. *Family Process, 23,* 561–569.

Isaacs, M.B. (1981). Treatment for families of divorce: A systems model of prevention. In I.R. Stuart & L.E. Abt (Eds.), *Children of separation and divorce: Management and treatment.* New York: Van Nostrand Reinhold.

Luepnitz, D.A. (1983). *Child custody: A study of families after divorce.* Lexington, Mass.: Lexington Books.

Messinger, L., & Walker, K.N. (1981). From marriage breakdown to remarriage: Parental tasks and therapeutic guidelines. *American Journal of Orthopsychiatry, 51*(3), 429–438.

Minuchin, S., & Fishman, C. (1981). *Family therapy techniques.* Cambridge, Mass.: Harvard University Press.

Montalvo, B. (1982). Interpersonal arrangements in disrupted families. In F. Walsh (Ed.), *Normal family process.* New York: Guilford Press.

Price-Bonham, S., Wright, D.W., & Pittman, J.F. (1983). Divorce: A frequent "alternative" in the 1970s. In E. Mackin & R. Rubin (Eds.), *Contemporary families and alternative lifestyles.* Beverly Hills, Calif.: Sage Publications.

Sager, C.J., Brown, H.S., Crohn, H., Engel, T., Rodstein, E., & Walker, L. (1983). *Treating the remarried family.* New York: Brunner/Mazel.

Schulman, G.L. (1981). Divorce, single parenthood and stepfamilies: Structural implications of these transactions. *International Journal of Family Therapy, 3*(2), 87–112.

Steinman, S. (1981). The experience of children in a joint-custody arrangement: A report of a study. *American Journal of Orthopsychiatry, 51*(3), 403–414.

Storm, C.L., & Sprenkle, D.H. (1982). Individual treatment in divorce therapy: A critique of an assumption. In E.O. Fisher & M. Fisher (Eds.), *Therapists, lawyers, and divorcing spouses.* New York: Haworth Press.

Wallerstein, J.S. (1983). Children of divorce: The psychological tasks of the child. *American Journal of Orthopsychiatry, 53*(2), 230–243.

Wallerstein, J., & Kelly, J. (1980). *Surviving the breakup: How children and parents cope with divorce.* New York: Basic Books.

Weiss, R.S. (1979). *Going it alone: The family life and social situation of the single parent.* New York: Basic Books.

8. Stages of Family Therapy with Severely Disturbed Adolescents

Susan K. Mackey

Audrey, a 17-year-old black adolescent, was referred for therapy following a two-week hospitalization at a private psychiatric facility. The hospitalization was precipitated by a psychotic episode in which Audrey had experienced auditory hallucinations of her dead grandmother and had acted in a paranoid manner. During this episode, she had seemed extremely withdrawn, frightened, and confused. There was no prior history of psychotic episodes. The parents reported that Audrey had always been "good," although she was not very active socially and had done poorly academically. Audrey's condition was diagnosed as paranoid schizophrenia, and antipsychotic medication was prescribed for her by the attending psychiatrist at the hospital. The family was referred for therapy by their health maintenance organization (HMO) in the hope that the therapist could provide "cost-effective" treatment for Audrey.

At first glance, an experienced family therapist might not consider this a difficult case. It would be simple to formulate the hypothesis that the girl's psychotic episode was related to a protective function in the family following the grandmother's death. There were several complicating factors in this case, however. First, several systems with conflicting viewpoints were involved: the parents, extended family members, the HMO, hospital personnel, the school, and the family's church. Second, the psychiatric diagnosis was very debilitating, and Audrey had been placed on medication that seriously impaired her functioning. Furthermore, because Audrey's mother was a psychiatric nurse, she was not likely to accept a challenge to this diagnosis. Third, the girl's poor functioning, both socially and academically, was now being interpreted in light of the diagnosis. Therefore, had the therapist challenged the diagnosis and reinterpreted the girl's behavior within a family framework, the family would have discredited the therapist and terminated the therapy.

Family therapy has been found to be effective with a wide range of problems (Borduin, Henggeler, Hanson, & Harbin, 1982; Dollinger, 1983; Frey, 1984; Gurman & Kniskern, 1978; Kraft & DeMaio, 1982; Krell, 1982; Levy & Brown, 1980–1981; Mirkin, Raskin, & Antognini, 1984; Rabkin, 1975; Weathers &

Liberman, 1975), in a wide variety of treatment settings (Borduin et al., 1982; Riche, 1983), and in various treatment modalities (Bruggen & Davies, 1977; Riche, 1983; Rubenstein, 1980). In addition, studies offer empirical support for the effectiveness of family therapy with adolescents (Borduin et al., 1982; Bruggen & Davies, 1977).

Despite the overall positive tone of the literature, a careful examination of the studies reveals limitations in both their methodology and their pragmatic usefulness to the clinician who is providing therapy to severely disturbed adolescents. For example, these studies rarely specify the treatment procedures in enough detail to permit specific clinical applications (Borduin et al., 1982). Even when treatment procedures are so specified, their effectiveness remains limited because of the flexibility and range of interventions needed in treatment, especially with difficult cases (Borduin et al., 1982). In addition, the long-term stability of short-term family therapy with severely disturbed adolescents has been questioned. Wellisch and Ro-Trock (1980) suggested that, while family therapy creates significant change, the change requires follow-up intervention to prevent deterioration of the results.

"Hard-to-treat" families include those with severely disturbed members, those with a variety of problems, and those with a prevailing defeatist attitude. Because the behavior of severely disturbed adolescents is embedded within several interrelated systems that can individually or jointly affect their behavior (Borduin et al., 1982), the therapist must adopt a broad view in which the relationship of these adolescents and their families to social systems is seen as the area of dysfunction (Kraft & DeMaio, 1982). Parents who have waited too long to attempt to intervene effectively with adolescents may have developed negative or defeatist attitudes (Frey, 1984; O'Connor & Horwitz, 1984). Even potentially effective strategies are rendered useless in these cases, because the adolescents have become inured to any change in their view of themselves or to the potency of any potential consequences of their actions. These attitudes also prevail when (1) attempts to have the parents take a united approach repeatedly fail, (2) the severity or frequency of the problem behavior escalates so quickly that it outweighs any consequences that might be delivered by the parents, and (3) the adolescents are so provocative as to convince others that change is impossible (O'Connor & Horwitz, 1984).

For the purposes of this article, the term *severely disturbed* refers to families with problems that

1. are severe in terms of the actual behaviors or in the rapidity with which these behaviors are escalating. Such behaviors are primarily self-destructive, harmful to others, or extremely and acutely socially inappropriate (e.g., psychotic episodes).

2. have resulted in a rigid definition or stance on the part of the adolescent, the family, or involved contexts such as school or legal systems (e.g., serious psychiatric diagnosis).
3. have continued for so long that very negative, defeatist attitudes prevail among the individuals involved with the adolescent.
4. stem from many different sources.

Family therapy is potentially very effective with adolescents, but unless the therapist recognizes the need for a broad, contextualized approach, its effectiveness is limited. The effectiveness will be further limited to the degree that the therapist is dealing with severely disturbed adolescents. Clinicians need a model to guide them through the course of therapy. A stage model allows an approach that can be individualized to the needs of the specific case while offering a process through which case decisions can be made. Although based within a structural-strategic theoretical framework, this approach makes it possible for the therapist to individualize the approach and to remain open to the use of techniques from a variety of orientations.

GUIDELINES

While the following guidelines may appear simplistic, they have a dramatic impact on the success of family therapy with severely disturbed adolescents.

Set realistic goals. The therapist should set subgoals in terms of small, realistic changes. It is better to be somewhat pessimistic in these difficult cases than to proceed too ambitiously and fail, thus damaging the future credibility of the therapist with this family and involved systems.

Look before leaping. The family often pressures the therapist to alleviate the problem quickly. The therapist must avoid the temptation to make hasty decisions, however, and must take the time to gather all relevant information and understand the viewpoints of all those involved in the problem (Borduin et al., 1982). Furthermore, it may take more than one session for family members to develop sufficient trust to be honest about their attitudes regarding the situation (Frey, 1984). In some situations, the therapist's attitudes may interfere with his or her ability to "hear" what the family is saying about the problem, particularly when the therapist's values and outlook are basically positive and the client's are negative. Further complicating the situation, the attitudes and values of the other systems involved, such as the referring person, must be considered as part of both the problem and the potential solution (Selvini-Palazzoli, Boscolo, Cecchin, & Prata, 1980).

Hedge all bets. Rarely should therapists take an unqualified stance, as they risk disqualification if they must later modify a stance or if they continue to insist on a stance that the family has firmly and repeatedly rejected. It is important for therapists to take a stance from which they can maneuver as they meet reactance or unforeseen circumstances in the course of therapy.

Remain alert to feedback. The obvious need to monitor feedback cannot be overemphasized for two reasons. One, these families are often pessimistic and may even have hidden agendas that the therapist cannot afford to overlook in his or her enthusiasm to create positive change within the family. Second, the therapist must determine the effects that interventions directed to one system exert on other systems related to the adolescent (Borduin et al., 1982). It is essential for the therapist to understand the complex changes and ramifications within the various contexts if therapy is to be successful.

Remain flexible. The therapist must be able to modify an approach or intervention strategy, if necessary, and to respond to various individuals within the involved systems in order to maintain their commitment to the treatment plan. At times, it may be most effective to conduct the family therapy through one person (Szapocznik, Kurtines, Foote, Perez-Vidal, & Hervis, 1983).

Prepare for all encounters. Therapy for families with a severely disturbed adolescent is fraught with crisis situations in which the therapist is called on to make instantaneous decisions. Unless the crisis is one for which the therapist and the family have prepared, however, the therapist must be careful about responding extemporaneously. Even in a true crisis situation, the therapist can usually ask for a brief period (even 10 minutes) to prepare a response. This time allows the therapist to refer to the therapy plan or even to consult with a colleague so as to avoid responding inappropriately. Obviously, the therapist must respond at once if there is any risk of immediate harm to the client or others, but the therapist should already have prepared a response to these situations. For example, the therapist not only must make clear his or her understanding of the seriousness of the situation and empathy for the individual's panic, but also must explain the need to make a good decision in such a crucial situation. This empathy is extremely important in the direct treatment of the adolescent.

STAGES

Once cognizant of the general guidelines, the therapist can plan the therapy in terms of a seven-stage process. It is only through proper preparation at each stage that the therapy can continue to proceed successfully.

Stage 1: Entering the Family and Establishing a Working Alliance

In the first stage, the therapist has two central tasks: (1) to gain the family's acceptance and cooperation, and (2) to obtain permission to proceed to Stage 2. Certain aspects of this stage resemble the moves of joining in structural family therapy, but the therapist must proceed in a much slower, more cautious fashion with a family that has a severely disturbed adolescent in order to determine the family's view of the problem first. Unless the therapist communicates a clear understanding of the problem and establishes a clear alliance with the family, therapy will not proceed effectively (Levy & Brown, 1980–1981; McPherson, Brackelmanns, & Newman, 1974). When these tasks have been accomplished, the family will grant the therapist permission to gather the information necessary to proceed. This can take more than one session.

> Audrey's parents were asked to attend the initial session with her and to bring Audrey's younger sister, Lu Ann (aged 10). At first, the parents expressed concern about Audrey's future and wanted immediate assistance in having her placed in a therapeutic school through the school district. Audrey, extremely lethargic because of the medication, participated little in the initial session.
> The mother was the family "expert" on the girl's "disease" and emotional needs. She also expressed concern about the impact of Audrey's behavior on Lu Ann. The therapist accepted the mother as an expert, but wondered at the same time if this led her to be very protective of her children. The parents agreed, and the father began to question whether this was always in Audrey's best interests, alluding to the domineering role her mother still played in his wife's life. The father was then framed as the practical parent who pushed for his children's independence and achievements.
> At the end of the initial session, the parents granted the therapist permission to talk with school personnel, the hospital staff, and the referring psychiatrist from the HMO. The parents were urged to contact the school on their own to arrange as soon as possible for a meeting with district personnel.

Stage 2: Collecting Information

Many people are involved when a family with a severely disturbed adolescent seeks therapy, and they may disagree about the definition and/or severity of the presenting problem. In order to have any success, the therapist must establish some mutually agreed upon starting position.

Each key participant should have an opportunity to express an opinion about the case individually; therefore, it is preferable to contact each separately before holding any joint meetings. Armed with an awareness of the various viewpoints of the participants, the therapist can begin to prepare a working reality that will be acceptable to all of them. With this preparation, joint meetings can be more productive.

The therapist should note which participants are considering residential placement as the solution to the problem and how rigidly they hold this stance. If the therapeutic plan is to maintain the adolescent in the home, placement must be forestalled. Sometimes, a moratorium on placement buys the therapist needed time. If the other key participants all agree that residential placement is the solution, the therapist's only alternative is to accept the inevitable and to work toward an acceptable plan that includes placement.

The therapist should also explore the history of the development of the problem. This helps the therapist to assess how longstanding the problem is, how defeated the participants feel, and what solutions have been attempted earlier so that the therapist will not proceed naively along a course of action already deemed a failure. Finally, the therapist should assess the ability of each participant to contribute to the solution of the problem.

The views of key participants may be organized in a grid format. The left-hand column is a list of the problems, and there is a place to indicate the level at which each participant listed across the top perceives the severity of that problem. Exhibit 8–1 is the completed information grid developed over three sessions with Audrey.

The key participants in Audrey's case identified three main problems: psychotic behavior, social isolation, and poor school achievement. All participants agreed that Problem 1 should be targeted at this stage. The hospital personnel recommended placement in a therapeutic facility. Audrey's mother, who also saw this behavior from a disease model, agreed. Although her father overtly agreed with his wife, he was less committed to the idea.

The HMO, acting primarily from financial considerations, did not support this placement and would not pay for four therapy sessions per week as recommended by hospital personnel. While seeing the problem as serious, the psychiatrist in charge of referrals at the HMO supported a practical, problem-solving approach. Hospital personnel were displeased with this decision, but recognized the HMO's financial constraints; under the circumstances, they were relieved to have no further responsibility for the case and to leave any further decisions to the therapist. This agreement was reached by contacting the respective participants individually. A joint meeting would undoubtedly have resulted in an unproductive and heated controversy that would have left the parents and therapist in the middle.

The parents were prepared to focus most of their energies on persuading the school system to assume responsibility for treatment by placing Audrey residentially, as recommended by hospital personnel. School personnel, hampered by procedural policies, took a defensive stance. The therapist, at this point, wanted to postpone any decision about placement in order to involve the parents in therapy. The therapist suggested to the parents that, since place-

Exhibit 8-1 Information Grid Developed in the Case of Audrey

Problem	Perceived Severity	M	F	A	SIB	OFM	TH	REF HMO	Court	Peer	Cult Church	School	Hospital
Problem 1: Psychotic behavior	Low												
	High		X	X	X	X	X	X	N/A	X	X	X	
	Placement	X											X
	Unknown												
Problem 2: Social isolation	Low	X	X	X		X							X
	High		X		X		X		N/A	X	X	X	X
	Placement												
	Unknown							X					
Problem 3: Poor school achievement	Low			X	X					X			
	High	X	X			X	X	X			X	X	X
	Placement												
	Unknown												

Participants

ment was unlikely before the end of the year, they should focus their energies on a realistic school plan for the remaining school year. School personnel were relieved and, therefore, willing to cooperate actively with the therapist. Before the actual meeting, the therapist coached the school personnel on "how to deal with these parents" and the parents on "how to deal with the school." When the actual meeting took place, verbal cues to each side were sufficient to control the content of the meeting.

Stage 3: Creating a Flexible Working Reality

Without a workable reality that all participants can actively support, the therapist should not proceed. The workable reality is essential; it is the overall framework within which the specific goals are set, and it provides a central theme to which the therapist can return when difficult points are encountered in the course of therapy.

The process of creating a workable reality is recursive. The therapist introduces a potential workable reality, presents it to the various participants, reads the feedback, refines the reality as needed, and re-presents it. During this tedious and sometimes discouraging process, patience is obviously essential. Throughout this process, the therapist should attempt to control and direct the flow of information personally so that the various participants do not talk directly to one another and thereby undermine the emerging workable reality.

It is crucial that each workable reality be individually tailored to the particular family and involved participants. In addition, the therapist should (1) focus on pragmatics, (2) avoid an overly optimistic stance, and (3) avoid involvement in disputes over rigid definitions. In general, it is easier for the various participants to agree on a pragmatically grounded workable reality. Furthermore, individual participants can back down from rigid stances with less loss of face if it is done in the service of a pragmatic necessity. Whenever workable realities can be presented in terms of alternatives, the participants are more likely to accept them.

For Audrey's mother, "reality" was limited by her definition of schizophrenia: a disease necessitating medication and a protected environment. This view limited the therapist, who saw little chance that Audrey would become more competent while medication or residential placement restricted her functioning. Given her mother's nursing background and the support her mother's definition had received from others, particularly the hospital personnel, it would have proved futile to challenge this definition overtly. Instead, the therapist painted for the parents a picture of two possible life styles open to their child. In the first, they would accept her limitations, maintain her on medication, and care for her in residential placement for her remaining life. In the second, they would explore their child's potential to lead a normal life. The therapist pointed out that the second alternative required the parents to help Audrey learn to manage her symptoms without medication and alluded to long-term side-effects of the medication. The therapist acknowledged that the second alternative not only required greater effort, but also included no guarantee of success. One strength was the mother herself, however; as a nurse, she was already an expert in dealing with psychotic symptoms.

Stage 4: Translating the Workable Reality into Goals

Three sets of goals must be articulated: overall case goals, session-by-session goals, and specific intervention goals within each particular session. At this stage, emphasis should be on the overall case goals that will guide the therapy. Pragmatic goals should be defined by the therapist, presented to the family, and translated into structural objectives to be achieved in a step-by-step progression. Table 8–1 illustrates the relationship between the symptomatic/pragmatic and structural goals in the case of Audrey.

Table 8–1 Therapeutic Goals for Audrey

Symptomatic/Pragmatic	Structural
1. Decrease medication.	1. The parents agree to the goal of managing symptoms without medication. This draws a boundary around the parental subsystem.
2. Increase age-appropriate behavior academically and socially at school.	2. The parents continue to function together.
3. Predict/reinforce parents' management of relapse (1 and 2 continue).	3. The parents work together to set more realistic and age-appropriate expectations, which continues to reinforce the boundary around the parental subsystem and begins to differentiate the adolescent individually.
4. Reinforce the adolescent's attempts at individuation and age-appropriate behavior (2).	4. As the adolescent becomes less involved in the family, marital conflict may emerge. This can be predicted, and the parents should be warned against reinvolving the adolescent.
5. Deal with emerging marital conflict (2, 3, 4 remain active).	5. a) The therapist holds individual problem-solving sessions with the adolescent regarding both social skills and tension arising from marital conflict. b) Marital sessions are scheduled.
6. Help the identified patient and parents work with the school to set up an appropriate long-term school program.	6. The parents continue to function as their adolescent's advocate while dealing with their own problems separately.
7. Help the adolescent and family learn to use community resources to meet the adolescent's long-term needs.	7. The family negotiates the boundary between the family and outside systems effectively.

Stage 5: Following Through

The overall case goals of Stage 4 must be translated into concrete, session-by-session goals that are consistent with the terms of the workable reality and attainable within a session. Generally, it is best to limit the number of goals to be achieved at any one session to one or two. Then, within a given session, the therapist should articulate the intervention that will achieve the particular goal.

Divided into small steps this way, an extremely difficult case appears much more manageable. The difficult part is the integration of the various interventions, both with the family and with other participants. The more participants involved, the greater the creativity required to coordinate and integrate interventions (Kraft & DeMaio, 1982).

Maintenance of the working reality in this stage may involve individual meetings to remotivate various participants, continual watchfulness to predict crises, and modification of the reality. Although not inevitable, marital conflict may surface as the adolescent begins to be differentiated within the family system. The therapist, at this point, should gradually shift the emphasis from parental cooperation to marital cooperation. At the same time, the therapist should schedule individual sessions with the adolescent to help him or her to cope with the increasing tension between the parents without becoming reinvolved.

Occasionally, a major unpredicted crisis will totally disrupt the effectiveness of the workable reality that has been developed. The therapist must then modify the framework or develop an alternative working reality. These are most discouraging times, but they must be expected and met as a challenge if therapy is to be successful.

The goal of one session with Audrey's parents was for them to devise a plan to handle any relapses into psychotic behavior. They developed a list of Audrey's possible behaviors and strategies to handle these behaviors without involving the therapist in the discussion. School personnel, who often responded to Audrey in a very protective, infantilizing manner, were directed to contact the parents if Audrey had a relapse so that her parents could handle her behavior. The preparation and the existence of this plan allowed both parents and the school personnel to remain comfortable with the workable reality.

Under her parents' direction, Audrey was required to participate in social activities and to complete her homework. As she became successful, the parents began to question the original diagnosis. The therapist cautioned that all participants must remain vigilant in case of relapse, however. Over the course of therapy, as the parents worked together to develop plans for Audrey, they became more and more open about their own marital conflicts. Audrey was seen individually while the parents began to deal overtly with marital issues. When Audrey did experience a relapse during this phase, Audrey and her parents placed the "plan" into action, and the relapse was of short duration.

Stage 6: Moving beyond Family Therapy

Throughout the process of therapy, intervention must involve systems beyond the family and the individual adolescent. At Stage 6, these systems often become the focal point. Haley (1980) suggested that disturbed adolescents would behave normally as a result of structural changes within the family. However, this model suggests that even when structural goals have been accomplished, the adolescent may be ill-prepared to cope with outside systems. The therapist then must focus on preparing the adolescent to function outside the family or other structured context. This involves an assessment of the individual's personal, social, academic/job, and other life skills. The individual and the family must be taught to find and manage the resources within the community that offer the opportunity to learn these skills (Kraft & DeMaio, 1982).

Often, the adolescent now requires individual therapy (Levy & Brown, 1980–1981) that focuses on coping and problem-solving skills, the practical skills required to face life as a functioning "individual." The eventual long-term goals of having the adolescent "leave home" may be very unrealistic unless the individual has been prepared.

Audrey was referred to group therapy available through the school and was required to stay involved in a certain number of school activities. At the end of the school year, plans were made for her to enter a vocational program in the school district. The therapist spent more time alone with her, talking about her plans, and had the parents develop for her a "life-skills training program" (e.g., setting up a checking account) that was directed by her father. The therapist also helped the family continue to find appropriate support systems within the school and community to help them with their life skills training (e.g., a park district program on skills for job interviews).

Stage 7: Terminating

Therapy for families with a severely disturbed adolescent is rarely over in terms of complete success; rather, there is a gradual separation. These families and their adolescents should be allowed to return for brief consultations over a period of years as crises arise. The adolescent, parent, and/or family can best be helped at this stage by brief therapeutic encounters to support their strengths, rather than a return to their original intense involvement with therapy.

CONCLUSION

Cases involving severely disturbed adolescents are certainly among the most difficult. They are characterized by frequent crises, rigid definitions, pessimism, and multiple problems. They require a tremendous amount of commitment and energy from the therapist. A great deal of tedious legwork, patience, and flexibility are required. Families frequently drop out of therapy at a crucial stage, only to recontact the therapist when their situation has returned to ground zero. A stage model allows the therapist to break the therapy into manageable parts, however, and provides an opportunity to be successful in cases often defined as hopeless.

REFERENCES

Borduin, C., Henggeler, S., Hanson, C., & Harbin, F. (1982). Treating the family of the adolescent: A review of the empirical literature. In S. Henggeler (Ed.), *Delinquency and adolescent psychopathology: A family-ecological systems approach* (pp. 205–222). Boston: John Wright.

Bruggen, P., & Davies, G. (1977). Family therapy in adolescent psychiatry. *British Journal of Psychiatry, 131,* 433–477.

Dollinger, S. (1983). A case report of dissociative neurosis (depersonalization disorder) in an adolescent treated with family therapy and behavior modification. *Journal of Consulting and Clinical Psychology, 51*(4), 479–484.

Frey, J. (1984). A family/systems approach to illness-maintaining behavior in chronically ill adolescents. *Family Process, 23,* 251–260.

Gurman, A., & Kniskern, D. (1978). Research on marital and family therapy: Progress, perspective and prospect. In S. Garfield & A. Bergin (Eds.), *Handbook of psychotherapy and behavioral change: An empirical analysis* (2nd ed., pp. 817–903). New York: Wiley.

Haley, J. (1980). *Leaving home: The therapy of disturbed young people.* New York: McGraw-Hill.

Kraft, S., & DeMaio, T. (1982). An ecological intervention with adolescents in low-income families. *American Journal of Orthopsychiatry, 52*(1), 131–140.

Krell, R. (1982). Family therapy with children of concentration camp survivors. *American Journal of Psychotherapy, 36*(4), 513–522.

Levy, J., & Brown, R. (1980–1981). The uncovering of projective identification in the treatment of the borderline adolescent. *International Journal of Psychoanalytic Psychotherapy, 8,* 137–149.

McPherson, S., Brackelmanns, W., & Newman, L. (1984). Stages in the family therapy of adolescents. *Family Process, 13,* 77–94.

Mirkin, M., Raskin, P., & Antognini, F. (1974). Parenting, protecting, preserving: Mission of the adolescent female runaway. *Family Process, 13,* 77–94.

O'Connor, J., & Horwitz, A. (1984). The bogeyman cometh: A strategic approach for difficult adolescents. *Family Process, 23,* 237–249.

Rabkin, L. (1975). Countertransference in the extreme situation: The family therapy of survivor families. In L. Wolberg & M. Aronson (Eds.), *Group therapy: 1975—An overview* (pp. 164–174). New York: Stratton.

Riche, M. (1983). Integrating families into a healing community: The use of structural and strategic family therapy in a psychodynamically-oriented hospital. *Residential Group Care and Treatment, 1*(4), 67–84.

Rubenstein, D. (1980). Family psychiatry in psychosomatics: Problems of adolescence. *Psychotherapy and Psychosomatics, 33,* 112–121.

Selvini-Palazzoli, M., Boscolo, L., Cecchin, G., & Prata, G. (1980). The problem of the referring person. *Journal of Marital and Family Therapy, 6,* 3–9.

Szapocznik, J., Kurtines, W., Foote, F., Perez-Vidal, A., & Hervis, O. (1983). Conjoint versus one-person family therapy: Some evidence for the effectiveness of conducting family therapy through one person. *Journal of Consulting and Clinical Psychology, 51*(6), 889–899.

Weathers, L., & Liberman, R. (1975). Contingency contracting in families of delinquent adolescents. *Behavior Therapy, 6,* 356–366.

Wellisch, D., & Ro-Trock, G. (1980). A three-year follow-up of family therapy. *International Journal of Family Therapy, 2*(3), 169–174.

9. Has Family Therapy Reached the Stage Where It Can Appreciate the Concept of Stages?

Richard C. Schwartz

The acceptance or appreciation of any new discovery or innovation proceeds in stages. For example, the field of family therapy has passed through several stages of development and acceptance vis-à-vis the mental health professions. The acceptance of a model or school within the field of family therapy also proceeds through several stages. Finally, individual therapists go through predictable stages in their appreciation of a model or even of the entire field. These three levels of system—the field, a model within the field, and a therapist—all undergo similar developmental periods if they continue to grow.

THE STAGES OF DISCOVERY

The staging process that surrounds any new discovery or advance begins with the *essentialistic stage*. The proponents or discoverers of the advance, considering it the long-sought piece of understanding or technology that captures the *essence* of the phenomena under observation, may develop a technique based on this new understanding. Or, they may stumble on a technique that appears to contain the essence because it worked in a few instances and later generate theory to explain this success. In either case, the technique is then applied to all manifestations of the phenomena, regardless of timing, characteristics, or context. Since the adherents of the technique believe that it affects the essence of the target phenomena, they are no longer inclined to study the variations or subtleties of the target phenomena—variation is not important if the essence has been found. During this essentialistic stage, any failure is explained away as misapplication of the technique, a defect in the phenomena, or faulty documentation of outcome.

It seems that the length of this essentialistic stage depends primarily on the degree to which the technique or discovery is accepted by the larger system. The more the essentialists must defend their technique, the more they feel like an enlightened group, the less they are able to examine their discovery critically or realistically, and the longer the essentialistic stage lasts.

88

When some of the essentialists begin to recognize that the technique is not working in every case, the transitional stage begins. This stage is full of turmoil, with some former adherents vengefully attacking the technique, the theory, and its discoverers and remaining adherents defending their beliefs even more rigidly. The disenchanted feel duped. If the new technique cannot cure or change all, then it cannot tap the essence, and their search for the truth is not over. Some of these people may join the supporters of rival theories or drop out of the field.

Those who remain loyal to the technique may develop theoretical axioms to suggest that the technique still finds the essence, but only if certain steps are taken before and after its application. Thus, in this stage, the remaining essentialists begin to consider the concept of stages in relation to their technique, but develop a rigid, cookbookish manner. The remaining adherents religiously follow their new protocol on the stages of application, but again show little concern with ways in which this process might be modified according to variations in the phenomena or the context in which it is used. The technique has become more complex, but its users are no less essentialistic.

The *relativistic stage* may gradually emerge from the chaos or rigidity of the transitional stage. Those who remained interested in the technique, but were able to accept its lack of essentialistic power and were willing to test it, begin to recognize a pattern in the technique's effectiveness. For example, the technique may be useful in certain contexts, but not others; with certain ranges or variations of the phenomena, but not others; after, before, or in conjunction with certain techniques or events, but not others. Guidelines for the differential application of the technique are written and the limitations of the theory surrounding it accepted. The role of both theory and technique within the larger body of knowledge in the field is increasingly recognized. The practitioners become comfortable with the idea that variation is primary; essences are illusory (Gould, 1983). Hence, they accept that there is no universal technique or theory but rather modifications and combinations of techniques and theories that correspond to variation in phenomena. During this stage practitioners begin to see the "patterns that connect" their technique and theory with others that they once believed to be contradictory or incompatible.

During the relativistic stage, a sophisticated appreciation of the concept of stages is finally achieved. Issues of timing, context, limitations, and relationship to other techniques take the foreground in the discussion of the technique. Rather than being seen as the essential technique, it is viewed as one of many alternative interventions. In addition, variations in the target phenomena are deemed worthy of further study so that the technique or the theory behind the technique can be modified to fit them better. Because their belief in the value of their technique or theory is more modest, these anti-essentialists can explore other ideas and learn from other schools of thought.

The field of family therapy is an interesting case study because the unfolding of these stages can be observed at several levels: (1) the introduction of family therapy and systemic thinking into the field of psychotherapy, (2) the advent of new models or techniques in the field of family therapy, and (3) the exposure of a family therapy trainee to the ideas and techniques of a model of family therapy. At each of these levels, the process seems isomorphic, although it occurs at different rates.

THE FIELD OF FAMILY THERAPY

Because it began as an underground, radical movement within a hostile psychiatric establishment, the field of family therapy inevitably experienced a long and passionate essentialistic stage. In order to differentiate family therapy from mainstream thought and recruit converts, family therapy pioneers had to speak dramatically and in terms of extremes: "We are systemic/they are linear; we can cure all problems/they can cure none; we are the therapy of the people/they are for the wealthy; we are good/they are bad." During this stage these extremes were reflected in rigidity of theory and technique: "We do not work with a family unless all members are present," or "all problems are maintained by interactions within the current context."

As family therapy has become more widely accepted as a valid and reliable orientation to human problems, much of the extreme dogma and essentialistic thinking has abated. It is less necessary to differentiate the field through dramatic dichotomies because there are fewer attacks from the establishment, and more converts. The dangers now facing the field are those that any radical movement faces once it succeeds: family therapy is becoming co-opted by the establishment. As Minuchin observed,

> The psychiatric field has incorporated family therapy as a modality of treatment—without, of course, changing the diagnostic categories of individual patients. . . . This is the way society works. It coopted a movement that was challenging basic ways of thinking about human problems by making it official. (Simon, 1984, p. 30)

Thus, diluted nonsystemic versions of family therapy have emerged.

Members of the "old guard" like Minuchin may view this co-opting as the inevitable outcome of becoming comfortable, letting our guard down, and becoming self-critical. Perhaps some degree of co-opting is inevitable. But I hope that fear-of-co-opting does not lead to another extreme, essentialistic stage in the family therapy field.

Minuchin has lamented that, despite family therapy's new respect and popularity, systemic thinking has not yet permeated the administrative levels of the major mental health institutions. He sees this lack of impact as a major failure of the field of family therapy (Simon, 1984). This diagnosis may be premature, however. In its essentialistic stage, family therapy was unlikely to have much influence on major institutions, and it has only very recently moved into the transitional and relativistic stages. If the field can avoid being coopted or diluted and can continue its journey toward relativism, there may be more change in institutions before long. In addition, more and more people are enjoying the freedom of thought in the relativistic stage. As Haley (1984), one of the most radical of the pioneers, said recently,

> At one time I thought I had more freedom because I was an outsider. I didn't have to think in a restricted way like the insiders. Then I realized I was not free because I was not allowed to think like an insider if I was to be on the outside. (Simon, 1982, p. 36)

MODELS OF FAMILY THERAPY

Clinical and conceptual models within the field evolve in much the same way that family therapy itself has evolved. Madanes and Haley (1977) noted that "when a therapy solidifies into a school, it tends to create a formal method of working. The same set of procedures and techniques is applied to every case no matter what the problem" (p. 89). Such method-oriented models or schools are in an early essentialistic stage. Their adherents believe that one method or set of concepts captures the essence of family problems.

Minuchin (1984) eloquently described the process by which ideas became essentialistic trademarks in the family therapy field:

> The old timers knew that their private truths were only partial, and when they met around a cup of coffee, they gossiped about the beginnings and shared their uncertainties and hopes. But lo and behold, their institutions grew and they needed large buildings to accommodate all their students. Slowly, before anyone realized it, the buildings became castles with turrets and drawbridges, and even watchmen in the towers. The castles were very expensive and they had to justify their existence. Therefore, they demanded ownership of the total truth. (p. 88)

Today, many different castles still exist. In some cases, the inhabitants guard them with as much paranoid ferocity as ever and rarely venture out. The harbinger of a new stage of development, however, is the increasing numbers of excited antiessentialists who, having gone through the essentialistic stage with one model, have traveled far enough to see their castle in perspective and are living on the borders between conceptual kingdoms or are on pilgrimages among the castles.

The leaders of this group are unlikely to erect impenetrable castles of their own. Castle-building requires the charisma and the single-mindedness that comes with the belief that one "knows" while others do not, and this group of antiessentialists is beyond that stage. Indeed, they are handicapped by their inability to describe families in simple, unidimensional language or to recommend the use of all-purpose techniques. As Minuchin (1984) observed, "When I first began to teach family therapy, I did so with a deceptive simplicity. Today I talk a lot more about the complexities" (p. 68).

Those who have left their castles tend to use the language of stages. They may write less about the details of a specific intervention and more about the context or timing of its use. They are apt to link interventions from different schools in new ways and to create conceptual frameworks that permit such linkages, but are still recognized as only partial realities.

As whole models of family therapy are leaving the essentialistic stage of development, views of the family are moving toward increased differentiation and relativity. As the field matures, more is written about the variation among families and less about a universal family pattern against which all families are measured.

INDIVIDUAL FAMILY THERAPISTS

Because the "mind" of the field or model is the interaction of the minds of individual therapists, it is natural for most new therapists to start at the essentialistic stage. Most rational people are terrified at the prospect of their first clinical encounter with a family. It is understandable that novice therapists blindly adopt any model of therapy that provides a sense of direction and comfort before they enter the mystifying maze of family interaction. Furthermore, their first success is likely to trigger an essentialistic fervor for the model used, no matter the length of the trail of failures leading to that first success. Like the proverbial man with a hammer to whom everything looks like a nail, the trainee at this stage looks for and sees only those family interactions that support the model. The technique that leads to some success or fits the model is applied to any and every case that even vaguely seems appropriate.

Some therapists spend their lives in this essentialistic stage, particularly those who maintain close ties to trainers or advocates of a model that is frozen in an essentialistic stage. Others gradually begin to recognize the limits of the model and to question its essentialism. They begin to experiment with new concepts or techniques, although the original model may remain a home base to which they add any new discoveries. Thus, initial forays are likely to involve models that share some basic premises with the original. This period is often characterized by a combination of feelings, including distress at the loss of essentialistic moorings, tempered by a comforting sense that the original model was simply incomplete and will regain its omnipotence if expanded to include compatible pieces from other models.

Gradually, however, these therapists may be led by clinical data to near and even cross the boundaries of the original model. An unsettling period of conceptual anomie is the common result. At this point, the confused therapists may (1) retreat to the home base model and no longer look beyond its walls, endowing it with even more essentialistic power; (2) suddenly disavow the model in toto and convert to a rival approach; or (3) make an antiessentialistic leap in conceptual ability, recognizing the patterns that connect a wide range of apparently disparate models of therapy. This leap cannot be made until the therapist is able to live without the comforting idea that there exists a model of therapy that has the corner on essences, or even that there are essences that can be distilled. The development of family therapists who grow beyond their original training is usually characterized by a series of such conceptual crises and inspirations in this transitional stage.

Therapists who have gone through and emerged from the essentialistic stage are better equipped to see the patterns that connect families or models of therapy because they are more open to the whole range of phenomena. They see each family type, interaction sequence, concept, or technique as worthy of investigation. In biology, this attitude has been expressed by Gould (1983):

> The taxonomic essentialist scoops up a handful of snails in a single species, tries to abstract an essence and rates his snails by their match to this average. The antiessentialist sees something entirely different in his hand—a range of irreducible variation defining his species, some variants more frequent than others, but all perfectly good snails. (p. 12)

How can a therapist avoid becoming stuck in the essentialistic stage and at the same time avoid becoming overwhelmed by all the choices or variations in different models? It may seem as if one must choose between being rigidly wedded to a single model forever, or being a confused or wishy-washy eclectic. How can we train therapists so that they have direction, conviction, and success, but also can evolve beyond the essentialistic stage? It is my contention that this expansive, anti-essentialistic attitude is very difficult to teach. A novice trainee must be able to focus narrowly in the beginning in order to make sense of all the variation. Using a single model is useful at this stage. A trainee will only believe this model is not omnipotent after its limits are experienced first hand. As a trainer, I can hope to help trainees be open to that experience and give direction for the gradual expansion of their model.

Thus I believe that a trainee's movement from narrow essentialism to anti-essentialistic integration is a natural and often necessary process. This assumption has the following implications:

1. It is a mistake to introduce the novice clinician to a wide range of apparently disparate models of therapy.
2. Instead, it is most helpful initially to provide a clear, focused, and relatively narrow conceptual framework, since that is all most novices can tolerate.
3. The trainer's attitude, while presenting this framework, will have a great deal to do with whether the trainee remains locked into this framework or continues the process of conceptual growth.

If the trainer is stuck at the essentialistic stage it will be very difficult to encourage the trainee to ever go beyond it. If the trainer is not stuck however, he or she can help the trainee focus on and learn a clear model thoroughly, while also modeling a lack of chauvinism about that model and either introducing the trainee to or showing respect for other approaches, when the trainee seems ready to expand.

CONCLUSION

Increasingly, individual family therapists, models of family therapy, and the entire field of family therapy are moving beyond essentialism. The language of stages is now spoken and understood by a large number of family therapists. It is a language of flexibility, timing, context, and relationships among techniques and concepts.

REFERENCES

Gould, S.J. (December 1983). Of wasps and WASPS. *Natural History*, pp. 8–15.

Madanes, C., & Haley, J. (1977). Dimensions of family therapy. *Journal of Nervous and Mental Disease, 165*, 88–98.

Simon, R. (1982). Behind the one way mirror: An interview with Jay Haley. *Family Therapy Networker, 6*, 18–29, 58–59.

Simon, R. (1984). Stranger in a strange land: An interview with Salvador Minuchin. *Family Therapy Networker, 8*, 20–31, 66–68.

Index

A

Abelsohn, D., 64, 67
Abrons, C.R., 62, 63, 64
Access to all family members,
  65
Accommodation, 47
Actors, 44, 46
Ad infinitum stance, 28, 29
Aministrative aspects of therapy, 12
Ahistory, 3, 5, 42
Alexander, J., 3, 10
Alliances, 79
Antiessentialistic stage of concepts,
  91-92, 93, 94
Antognini, F., 75
Aponte, H.J., 41
Assessment process, 41
Attitudes
  defeatist, 76
  of therapist, 25

B

Baker, L., 41
Bardene, S.M., 9

Barrett, M.J., 44
Barthelme, Donald, 51
Barton, C., 3, 10
Bateson, G., 3
Beginning stage, 12, 16-25
  in strategic therapy, 51, 54
Behavioral therapy, 3, 4
Belief systems, 27, 28, 29,
  42
Bell, J.E., 8, 11
Benjamin, M., 62
Bernstein, B.E., 66
Bishop, D.S., 3, 4, 11
Bodin, A., 16
Borduin, C., 75, 76, 77, 78
Boscolo, L., 16, 47, 77
Boundaries, 8, 41, 42
  reformation of, 67
Brackelmanns, W., 79
Bray, G.P., 9
Brendler, J., 9, 26, 41
Breunlin, Douglas C., 1, 6,
  10, 16, 19, 43, 46
Brown, H.S., 72
Brown, R., 75, 79, 85
Bruggen, P., 76

C

Cantor, P., 9
Capra, F., 47
Carey, A., 9
Carl, D., 21
Cecchin, G., 16, 47, 77
Chabot, D.R., 9
Challenge, 24
Change
    consolidating and dealing with
        consequences of, 12
    creation of, 19-20
    envolving process of, 26-32
    initial attempt at, 12
    in middle phase, 27-32
    of perspective, 16
    process of, 8
    resistance to, 28
    timing of, 6, 7
Change agent role of therapist,
    47
Chronic vs. transitional problems,
    67
Cimmarusti Rocco A., 16, 19,
    43
Cleveland, M., 9
Clues, 46
Colapinto, J., 19, 24, 41, 42, 43
Combrinck-Graham, L., 9, 26, 41
Complementarity of relationships,
    43
Compromise, 66
Conceptualization, 44
Conflict resolution style,
    66
Consolidation
    of consequences of change, 12
    of gains, 47-48
Coogler, O.J., 66
Cox, M., 63
Cox, R., 63
Crisis situations, 55,
    78
Crohn, H.S., 72
Cybernetics, 5

D

Davies, G., 76
Defeatist attitudes, 76
Dell, P., 28, 29
DeMaio, T., 75, 76, 84, 85
Derdyn, A.P., 9
Development, 27, 28, 29, 31-32
Diagnosis, 19, 20
Differentiation, 70-71
Digital communication, 3
Digital therapy, 3
Directives. See Tasks
Discontinuity, 3, 5, 6-7
Divorcing families, 62-73
    framework for, 64
    structure of, 62
Dollinger, S., 75
Double vision, 19, 22

E

Ecology, 42
Emergency plan, 55
Emotionality, 66-67
Ending stage, 13, 33-40
    See also Termination
    in strategic therapy, 54
    in structural therapy, 48-49
Engel, H., 72
Eno, M., 68
Epstein, N.B., 3, 4, 11
Erickson, Milton, 35
Error in staging, 13
Essentialistic stage of concepts, 88, 90,
    91, 92, 93, 94
Envolving ecology, 42
Envolving process of change, 26-32

F

Facts, 18-19
Family dance, 42
Family mediation, 66
Faulkner, J., 9
Feedback, 19, 20, 44, 78

Fine, S., 9
Fisch, R., 16, 35, 47
Fishman, H.C., 16, 18, 24, 41, 42
   46, 64
"Fix it" mentality, 3
Flexibility, 78
   in scheduling, 36
   in working realities, 82-83
Foley, V.D., 9
Following through, 84
Foote, F., 78
Form (space), 42, 46
Fouts, J., 26
Frame of reference, 54
Freeman, D.S, 8, 10
Frey, J., 75, 76, 77
Friedricks, S., 11
Functional family therapy
   model, 3

G

Gains consolidation, 47-48
Gazda, G.M., 8, 11
Gelcer, E., 9
Generationally organized hierarchy, 27
Glass, D.R., 9
Goals, 16, 17, 20, 28, 53
   realistic, 77
   translation of workable realities
      into, 83
Goldsmith, J., 62, 63, 64
Goldstein, Sidney E., 16
Gould, S.J., 89, 93
Griffiths, J., 9
Gross, E., 8, 10
Gross, G., 9
Growth-oriented family therapy, 36
Gurman, A., 75
Gursky, E.J., 9, 26, 41
Guttman, H.A., 9

H

Haley, Jay, 3, 8, 10, 16, 27, 30, 35,
   37, 47, 51, 52, 54, 59, 85, 91

Hancock, E., 9
Hansen, J.C., 72
Hanson, C., 75
Harbin, F., 75
Hare-Mustin, R.J., 41
Harre, R., 40
Haynes, J.M., 66
Heard, D.B., 41
Heath, Anthony W., 33
Heatherington, E.M., 63
Henggeler, S., 75
Hervis, O., 78
Hierarchy, 27, 41
Hill, H.A., 9
History of family therapy,
   90-91
Hoffman, L., 3, 6, 41, 48
Holons, 42, 46, 47, 64
Hope, 24
Horwitz, A., 76
Hostility during sessions,
   66
Huberty, C.E., 9
Huberty, D.J., 9
Hypotheses, 22-23
   initial, 53

I

Individual therapy, 85, 92-94
Information collection, 79-82
Initial attempt at change stage, 12
Initial hypothesis, 53
In-session hostility, 66
In-session issues, 23-25
Intensity creation, 8, 17
Interactional diagnosis, 19, 20
Intervals between sessions, 38
Intervention, 44
Involvement level of therapist,
   54
Irving, H.H., 62, 66
Irwin, K., 9
Isaacs, M.B., 67
Isomorphism, 3, 5-6, 46

J

Jacobs, E., 11
Jeffrey, J., 9
Joining, 17, 19, 20, 24, 43,
   79
Joint custody of children, 62
Jurich, A.P., 9
Jurkovic, G.J., 21

K

Kantor, D., 11
Karrer, Betty M., 41
Kelly, J., 63, 64, 67
Kich, G.K., 9
Kniskern, D., 75
Kraft, S., 75, 76, 84, 85
Krell, R., 75
Kurtines, W., 78

L

Landau, J., 9
Lappin, Jay, 9, 16, 19, 24
Leaving Home, 3
Level of involvement of therapist,
   54
Levy, J., 75, 79, 85
Liberman, R., 76
Liddle, H.A., 6
Life cycle, 23, 27, 42
Luepnitz, D.A., 63, 67, 70

M

Mackey, Susan K., 75
Madanes, C., 41, 47, 91
Maintenance of working realities, 84
Marital dissolution phases, 67-70
Marital holon, 64
Mas, H., 3, 10
Mazza, Judith, 51, 57
McGuire, Dennis, 26
McPherson, S., 79
Mediation, 66

Medical practice model of therapy (MPMT)
   application of, 36-39
   termination in, 34-35
Mental Research Institute Brief Therapy
   Center, 35
Messinger, L., 70
Middle phase of therapy, 26-32
Minuchin, S., 16, 18, 24, 27, 41
   42, 43, 44, 45, 46, 48, 64, 90, 91, 92
Models of family therapy, 91-92
   See also specific models
Montalvo, B., 41, 63, 64
Morin, M., 75
Movement process, 41
MPMT. *See* Medical practice model of
   therapy
Mueller, P.S., 9
Music analogy, 4

N

Negative label intensification, 17
Neutrality of therapist, 65
Newman, L., 79

O

Observation, 44
O'Connor, J., 76
Onset of problem, 5
Organizational makeup of family, 30
Orlandis, M.M., 9
Other service providers, 17, 18, 21-22
Out-of-session issues, 21-23

P

Pace, 20
Palazzoli, M.S., 47
Papp, P., 47
Paradoxical strategies, 47, 48
Parental holon, 64
Parent-child holon, 64
Partial arc, 5
Patience, 25
Perez-Vidal, A., 78

Personal vulnerabilities of therapist, 29
Perspective change, 16
Pittman, J.F., 69
Planned termination, 37-38
Planning, 48, 49, 66, 67, 78
  disclosure of, 37
  emergency, 55
Positive connotations, 16, 17, 37, 54
Posture, 54
Powell, G.S., 8, 11
Pragmatic theapy, 3, 4
Prata, G., 16, 47, 77
Presenting edge, 5
Press, S., 39
Price-Bonham, S., 69
Problem-focused therapy, 3, 4, 35
Problem onset, 5
Problem redefinition (relabeling),
  16, 17, 54
Problem Solving Therapy, 3
Process, 42
  of change, 8
  language of, 3
  of movement, 41
Psychological deficits in families, 36

R

Rabkin, L., 75
Ransom, J.W., 9
Rapport, 54
Raskin, P., 39, 75
Readjustment, 72-73
Realistic goals, 77
Recovery phases, 70-73
Redifinition of problems (relabeling),
  12, 16, 17, 54
Reductionistic world view, 43
Reframing, 16, 54
Reintegration, 71-72
Relabeling (redefinition of problem),
  12, 16, 17, 54
Relativistic stage of concepts, 89, 91
Resistance, 41
  to change, 28
Restructuring, 47

Riche, M., 76
Rodstein, E., 72
Rohrbaugh, M., 39
Rossman, B.L., 41
Ro-Trock, G., 76
Rubenstein, D., 76

S

Saba, G., 6, 44
Sager, C.J., 72
Sakamoto, Y., 9
Sander, N., 9
Satir, V., 16
Scheduling flexibility, 36
Schilling, S.M., 8, 10
Schlesinger, S., 9
Schneider, T., 11
Schonitzer, D.L., 11
Schulman, G.L., 68
Schwartzman, John, 41
Schwartz, Richard C., 6, 17, 44, 46,
  48, 88
Searching for clues, 46
Segal, L., 35
Self-regulation, 47
Selvini-Palazzoli, M., 16, 34, 77
Sequencing of events during divorce,
  63
Serritella, D., 9
Severely disturbed
  adolescents who are, 75-86
  defined, 76
Sexual role sterotyping, 41
Sibling holon, 64
Simon, R., 90, 91
Simons, Virginia A., 62
Slavek, N., 11
Sluzki, Carlos, 9, 17
Social systems, 42
Social unit, 54
Sociocultural beliefs, 42
Solomon, M.A., 8, 10
Southbeach Psychiatric Center, Staten
  Island, New York, 44
Space, 42, 46

Spatial dimensions of staging process,
    42, 44, 49
Sprenkle, Douglas H., 9, 62, 67
Stages
    of divorcing family therapy, 62-73
    of strategic family therapy, 51-61
    of structural family therapy, 41-49
    of therapy with severely disturbed
        adolescents, 75-86
Staging, defined, 4
Staging error, 13
Stanton, M.D., 41
Steinglass, P., 41
Steinman, S., 62, 67
Stereotypic sexual roles, 41
Storm, C.L., 9, 67
Strategic family therapy, 26
    stages in, 51-61
Strategy, 53
Structural family therapy, 17, 18, 26
    stages of, 41-49
    theoretical assumptions of, 42-43
Structure, 27, 28, 29, 30-31
    of divorcing families, 62
Systematic approach, 27
Systems theory, 5, 6, 43
Szapocznik, J., 78

T

Talmon, M., 41
Tasks (directives), 16, 17, 20, 53
    purposes of, 53
Temporal dimensions of staging
    process, 42, 44, 46-49
Tennen, H., 39
Tension during sessions, 66
Termination
    See also Ending stage
    defined, 35
    in medical practice, 34-45
    planned, 37-38
    in structural therapy, 48-49
    in therapy with severely disturbed
        adolescents, 85
    unplanned, 33, 38-39

"Terminations, " 35
"Therapist will fix it" mentality, 3
Therapy, defined, 35
Time, 42, 46, 47
    between sessions, 38
Timing, 20
    of change, 6, 7
    of events during divorce, 63
    of therapy, 5
Todd, T., 41
Tolerance, 25
    of emotionality, 66-67
Tomm, K., 38
Too-compromising stance, 28
Transitional vs. chronic problems, 67
Transitional stage of concepts, 89
Treatment plan disclosure, 37
Trocine, N., 62
Truth, 18-19

U

Umbarger, C.C., 26, 41
Uncompromising stance, 28
Unplanned termination, 33, 38-39
Usher, M.L., 9

V

Van Deusen, J., 41
Variables for defining stage, 53-54
Vass, M., 11
Viewers, 44, 46
Vore, D.A., 9
Vulnerabilities of therapist, 29

W

Waldron, H., 3, 10
Walker, K.N., 70
Walker, L., 72
Wallerstein, J.S., 63, 64, 67, 72
Watzlawick, P., 16, 35, 47
Weakland, J.H., 16, 35, 47
Weakland, T., 16
Weathers, L., 75

Weiss, R.S., 71
Wellisch, D., 76
Whitehead, A.N., 6
White, L., 39
Wolkenstein, A.S., 9
Wood, B., 41
Woody, J.D., 9
Workable realities, 16, 17, 18-20, 21,
   43, 44, 45, 46-47, 49, 79
   family acceptance of, 20
   flexibility in, 82-83
   maintenance of, 84
   translation of into goals, 83

Working alliance, 79
Working with other service providers,
   17, 18, 21-22
Working realities. *See* Workable realities
World view
   of family, 46
   reductionistic, 43
Wright, D.W., 69
Wright, L. 9

Z

Zinner, J., 9